Editor Lis Edwards
Designer Mick Hodson
Production Susan Mead

Acknowledgements

Graham Allen Front cover
Janet Blakeley/N E Middleton Ltd 36–37, 40–41
Wendy Bramall/Artist Partners Ltd 8–9, 14–15,
20–21, 26–27, 32–33
Hayward Art Group Back cover
David Hurrell/N E Middleton Ltd 7, 38–39
Cynthia Pow/N E Middleton Ltd 22–23, 30–31
Steve Rigby 10–11, 12–13, 16–17, 18–19, 24–25,
28–29, 34–35

Endpaper photograph Heather Angel

Front cover: Oystercatchers and their nest on a
sandy shore

Endpapers: Low tide on a sheltered shore

First published 1981
Reprinted 1983
Macdonald & Co. (Publishers) Ltd
Holywell House
Worship Street
London EC2A 2EN

Printed in Hong Kong

ISBN 0 356 07123 5

LIFE ON THE SEASHORE

David Gilman

Macdonald

Contents

Exploring the seashore

Exploring the seashore

This book is all about the seashore – the tiny strip of land at the edge of the sea. Thousands of animals and plants live there, hidden under the sand, in rock pools, even in the dry seaweeds at the top of the beach. Some are large and easy to find, others are so small that you have to hunt for them. Each has its own fascinating way of life.

What is a seashore?

The shore reaches from the point covered by the highest spring tide to the point uncovered by the lowest spring tide.

To most people 'seashore' means a sandy beach, but there are many other kinds of shore. A seashore may be a salt-marsh, with the sea creeping slowly in over the mud, a shingle beach with rolling pebbles, or a steep cliff, where the waves crash against the rocks.

All seashores have one thing in common. The plants and animals there once lived in the sea, so when they are uncovered by the tide their unprotected bodies begin to dry up. Some plants and animals have become adapted to living in the drier, upper-shore regions, while others must live lower down the shore in the wetter areas.

Living on a seashore

Plants and animals have developed many different ways of coping with the problems of life on a seashore. Some, like fishes, live underwater all the time and would die quickly out of water. Others live underwater part of the time but can live out of water for short periods, like crabs and many seaweeds.

Others are land animals or plants which can only live near the sea. Seabirds, such as gulls, build their nests on cliffs or sand dunes, and feed on fish and molluscs. There are many plants, like sea holly, which need salty air or sandy soil.

On each different kind of seashore you will find different animals and plants. Some live in rocky hollows, which hold sea-water between tides. Others live buried under the sand, where it is always damp. Each animal or plant is specially adapted to living where it does. Some have suckers to hold on to rocks, others have filters to keep sand out of their breathing tubes.

This book shows you where to look for animals and plants on different types of shore, and helps to identify what you find. It also explains some of the many ways in which animals and plants live together, here at the edge of the sea.

◀ Rock pools are full of fascinating plants and animals, and are great fun to explore.

Sandy shores

Sand is easily moved about by the wind and the waves. The surface sand dries up quickly when the tide is out, so there are very few safe places for plants and animals to live.

Burrowing animals

Most sandy shore animals live under the sand. They are protected from the waves, and the sand stays firm and damp, even when the tide is out.

The lugworm (23) lives in a U-shaped burrow. The worm coats the inside of the tube with sticky mucus to stop it from collapsing. It feeds by swallowing sand and digesting the food it contains. The sandy worm-casts are easy to find when the tide is out.

The ragworm (22), more common on muddy shores, also lives in a slime-lined burrow, which it leaves to find food.

Most sea-anemones live on rocks. There are few rocks on sandy shores, but one anemone (17) has overcome the problem by living in a burrow. Only its feeding tentacles lie on the surface, and these are withdrawn into the burrow at any disturbance.

◄ Jellyfish life cycle

The larva (1) attaches itself to a rock. The body grows (2), producing 16 tentacles (3). The body divides into a pile of discs (4). The discs grow tentacles and swim away (5). Each grows into an adult jellyfish.

Adult jellyfish
Swimming larva (summer)
Grows attached to a stone (winter)
Divides into discs (spring)

Feeding tentacles and gills

Shell

Gravel

Sand

Bristle-legs

◄ Sandmason

The sandmason makes its long, delicate, untidy tubes from sand, small stones or bits of shell. It glues the pieces together with slime. The worm moves up and down inside the tube using 17 pairs of bristle-legs.

8

A burrowing fish

The sand-eel (36) burrows into fine, clean sand using its long, extendable jaws. The wet sand keeps the eel moist when the tide is out. It also hides the sand-eel from birds or larger fish looking for a tasty meal.

Key

1 Jellyfish	14 Daisy anemone	27 Catworm
2 Sandmason tubes	15 Tellin	28 Pod razor
3 Dogfish egg-case	16 Sandmason	29 Burrowing sea-cucumber
4 Herring gull	17 Burrowing anemone	30 Sea-potato
5 Lugworm casts	18 Netted dogwhelk	31 Sand gaper
6 Sea radish	19 Common starfish	32 Bootlace worms
7 Sandhoppers	20 Necklace shell	33 Sea-mouse
8 Barnacles	21 Burrowing starfish	34 Masked crab
9 Periwinkles	22 Ragworm	35 Cockle
10 Serrated wrack	23 Lugworm	36 Lesser sand-eel
11 Mussels	24 Purple heart-urchin	37 Rayed trough shell
12 Eel grass	25 Sword razor	38 Striped venus shell
13 Wedge shell	26 Peacock worm	39 Sand goby

▲ Sandhoppers

Sandhoppers are very useful as they eat all kinds of decaying matter – like seaweed and dead crabs. They hop by pushing against the ground with their tails and suddenly straightening their bent bodies.

Buried bivalve molluscs

The razor shell (25), (28), the cockle (35) and sand gaper (31) live buried in the sand. They are connected to the surface by two tubes called 'siphons'. One brings food and water to the body. The other pumps out water and waste.

▶ Eel grass

Eel grass is one of the few flowering plants that live in the sea. A whole community of animals can live and feed in the safety of its long stems and creeping roots. The roots also help to bind the sand together.

▲ Key	
1 Shore crab	5 Sea slug
2 Lugworm	6 Pod razor
3 Topshell	7 Sand-eel
4 Cockle	8 Burrowing anemone
	9 Periwinkle

Starfishes, sea-urchins, sea-anemones

Starfishes and sea-urchins belong to the Echinoderms ('spiny-skinned'). They have chalky plates under the skin, and move on tube-feet.

Sea-anemones have no skeletons. Their bodies have a sucker at the bottom.

* Not to scale. Average size given.

▲**Cushion star** 2-4cm diameter
This small browny-yellow or green starfish is found under stones on the lower shore. Its rough, stiff body has five short arms with rounded tips, and looks rather like an old-fashioned pincushion.

▲**Common sunstar** 15-25cm diameter
The sunstars live in the sea but may be washed up. They have from ten to fourteen blunt-ended arms. This one looks like a flaming sun. It feeds on oysters, mussels and other starfish.

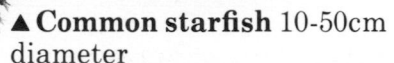

▲**Common starfish** 10-50cm diameter
Often found on the lower shore in mud, sand and rocky pools. Its colour varies from brownish-yellow to purple. It eats mussels and oysters, which it pulls open with its tube-feet.

Test

Test

▲**Green sea-urchin** 5-6cm
This prickly animal lives on the lower shore. Its green spines have purple tips. It disguises itself with pieces of seaweed or small stones which stick on to the spines. The empty shell, called a **test**, is also green.

▲**Sea-potato** 10cm
A common sea-urchin, which burrows to a depth of 15cm in clean sand. It often lives in groups in the middle and lower shore. The test looks like a potato.

▲**Common brittle-star** 12cm diameter (top) **Burrowing brittle-star** up to 30cm diameter (bottom)
Common on the lower shore of sandy beaches or among rocks. The burrowing brittle-star has very long arms and burrows in the sand. Look for the five rows of spines on the common brittle-star. The arms are easily broken but will slowly regrow.

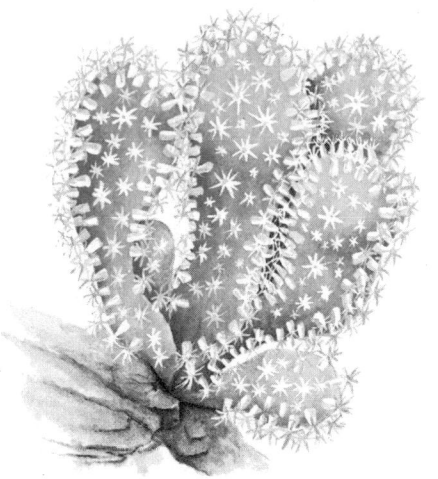

▲ **Dead men's fingers** 20cm high
These animals are halfway
between anemones and corals.
Each of the flesh-coloured
branches contains many
anemone-like animals. They have
jellyish bodies, which are held up
by chalky rods.

Sea-anemones

Beadlet anemones are very
common on rocks and in pools
on rocky shores. There are red,
green and strawberry forms, all
with 24 bright blue spots at the
top of the body. Their stinging
tentacles can poison even a
small fish.

Out of water, sea-anemones look
like blobs of jelly. They pull in
their tentacles and trap water to
stop them drying up.

Sea-anemone
out of water

Strawberry
beadlet
anemone

Red beadlet anemone

Sea-anemone
catching a fish

▲ **Snakelocks anemone** 10cm
high
Lives in shallow, sunny rock pools
on the middle and lower shore. It
is a dull green-brown, and has 200
purple-tipped tentacles. They
wave about like tiny snakes, and
cannot be completely withdrawn.

▲ **Dahlia anemone** 15cm high
This large anemone hides among
the rocks, stones and weeds in the
middle and lower shore pools. It
often attaches bits of shell, gravel
or weed to the sticky grey warts on
its body for camouflage.

▲ **Daisy anemone** 10cm high
This trumpet-shaped anemone
lives in rocky crevices or buried in
mud on the lower shore. It
withdraws out of sight if
disturbed. There are about 750
short, spotted tentacles.

▶ **Hermit crab anemone** 8cm
high
This anemone usually lives on the
shells of large hermit crabs,
although it can live on rocks. It
eats scraps of food left by the crab.
The anemone protects the crab
with its stinging tentacles.

▲ **Burrowing anemone** 10cm
high
This worm-like anemone burrows
in sand and mud for protection.
The body has 12 stripes running
from top to bottom. There are 12
pointed tentacles, with arrow-
shaped marks at their bases.

Worms and jellyfishes

There are many fascinating seashore animals hiding on a beach. Burrowing worms are easy to find. Look for wormcasts on sand and mud. These show the positions of their burrows. Sponges and tube-worms are common on the lower parts of the shore.

Jellyfishes are often stranded on the beach as the tide goes out. You may also find hornwrack and sea-mat left behind by the tide.

* Not to scale. Average body length given.

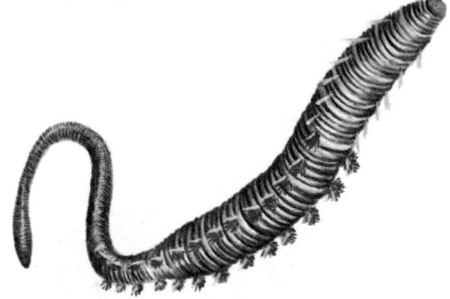

▲ **Lugworm** 20cm
A common worm which lives in U-shaped burrows in sand and mud, from the middle shore downwards. The soft, plump body has red feathery gills. Fishermen dig lugworms up for bait.

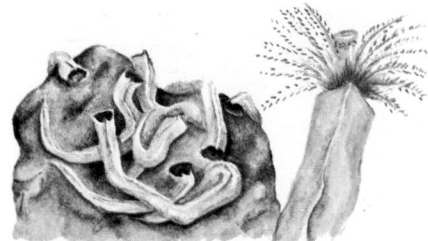

▲ **Keelworm** 2.5cm tube 5-6cm
These common worms make twisting chalky tubes on rocks and shells. On the top is a ridge or 'keel'. When it is underwater, the worm puts out a crown of red and white gills, with which it catches food.

▲ **Ragworm** 12cm
A common worm which burrows in sand and mud in the middle and lower shores. Its colour varies from orange to green. Look for the red blood-vessel running down its back. It has over 100 bristly segments.

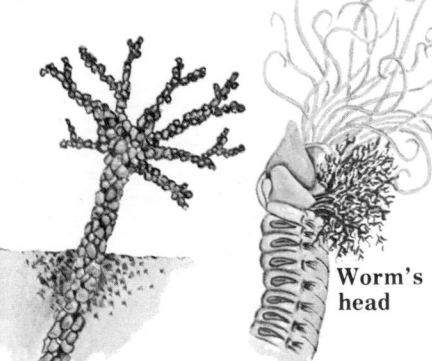

Worm's head

▲ **Sandmason** 30cm
You may see tiny tubes sticking out of the sand or mud at low tide. Some are the homes of sandmasons. These worms build fragile tubes out of tiny grains of sand, gravel, or shell, stuck together with slime.

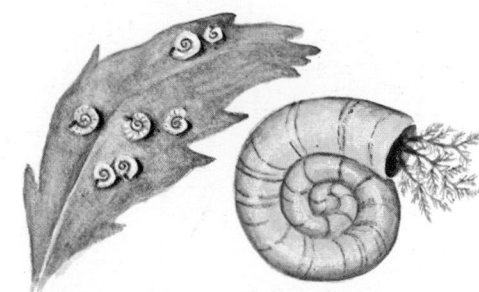

▲ **Spirorbis** diameter 35mm
A worm which lives in tiny chalky tubes on the fronds of brown seaweeds, oarweeds, rocks and stones. When the tide is out, the worm closes the end of the tube with a tiny chalky flap to trap water inside.

▲ **Green leaf worm** 5-15cm
This bright green worm is common in rock pools in the middle and lower shore. It swims about, using its large bristles as paddles. At low tide it creeps over rocks, feeding on barnacles.

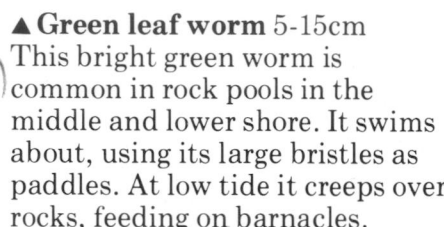

▲ **Peacock worm** 25cm
The brightly coloured peacock worm also lives in a tube. When covered by water the animal moves up its tube and strains food from the water with its gills. At low tide the tube traps water, so the worm can keep wet.

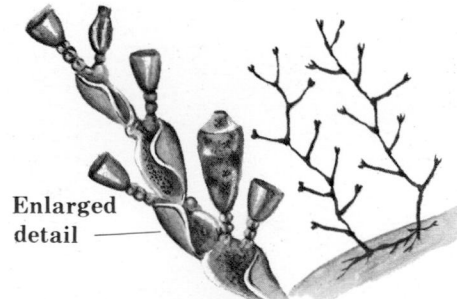

Enlarged detail

▲ **Obelia** 4cm high
Found on brown seaweeds and oarweeds. The tiny zigzag stems look like plants, but each branch contains a tiny, anemone-like animal. The upright 'stems' are connected by creeping root-like tubes.

▲ Sea-mouse 10-20cm

This strange, flat, oval-shaped worm is covered with fine hairs which are brilliant green and gold. It usually lives offshore but may be found in lower shore pools. Sea-mice are often washed up on the beach.

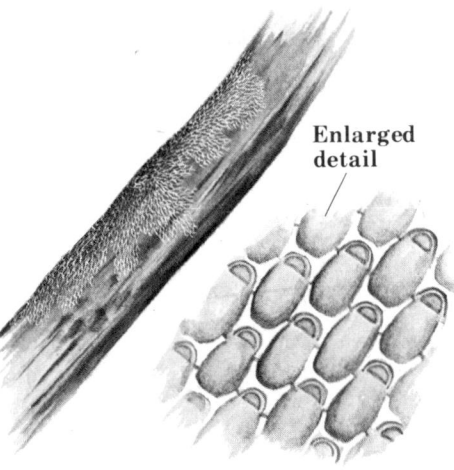

Enlarged detail

▲ Sea-mat

You may see small whitish patches on brown seaweeds and oarweed. With a hand lens you will see that each is made of tiny white boxes. Each box contains a minute animal, living inside a chalky 'shell'.

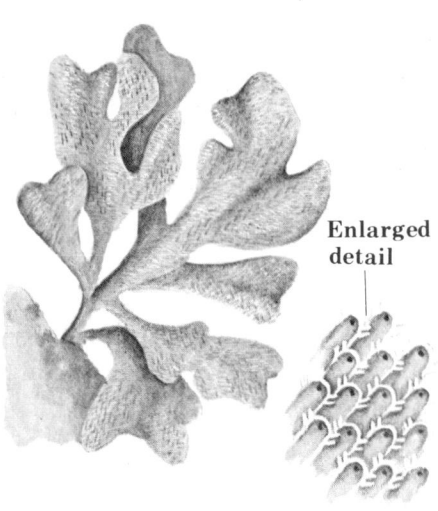

Enlarged detail

▲ Hornwrack 20cm

Like the sea-mat this is a group of animals, each living in a tiny chalky box. Colonies form a shape like a flat plant. They live in deep water, but when dead are often washed up on beaches.

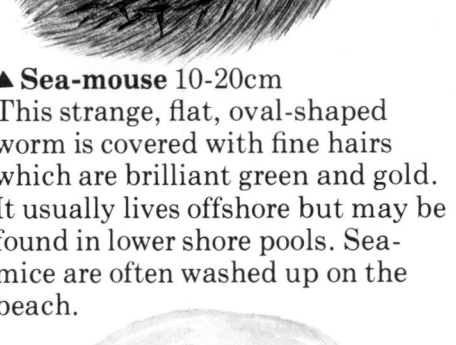

▲ Common jellyfish diameter 25cm

This common animal floats in shallow sheltered water like a transparent umbrella. On top are four violet, horseshoe-shaped marks (its reproductive organs), and four mouth arms hang below.

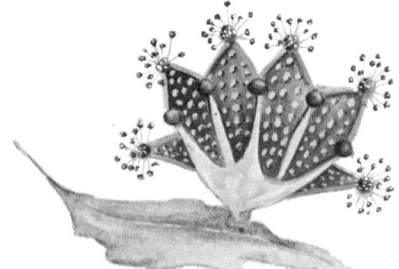

▲ Stalked jellyfish 5cm high

A tiny trumpet-shaped jellyfish with eight bunches of knob-like tentacles around the edge of its body. It usually stays in one place, attached to seaweeds in pools on the lower shore, but sometimes swims or floats.

▲ Portuguese man-o'-war 15-30cm

This jellyfish has a gas-filled bladder which floats. Long tentacles trail underneath, catching food. Some have dangerous stinging cells.

Sponges

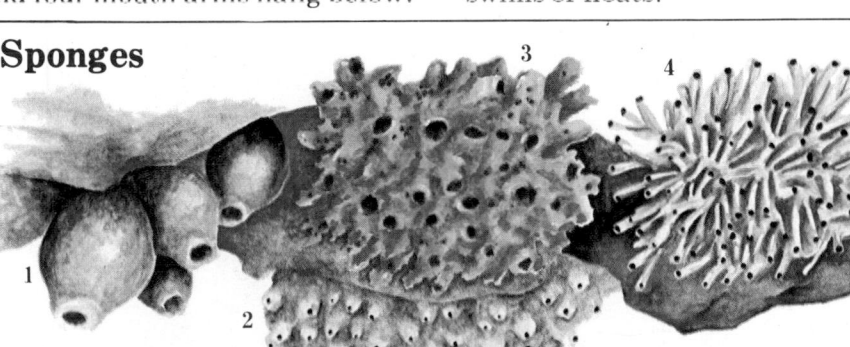

Sponges live on the lower shore. They are colonies of single cells inside a soft covering supported by tiny splinters of chalk or silica.

1 Purse sponge: 3-5cm long. Hangs down on the underside of rocks.

2 Breadcrumb sponge: Like a piece of green foam-rubber.

3 Myxilla: A cushion-like sponge on rocks and sometimes on spidercrabs.

4 Leucosolenia: Often attached to seaweeds.

A rock pool

Rock pools come in all shapes and sizes. Each is a tiny world full of fascinating animals and plants. What you find in a rock pool will vary a great deal, depending on its level on the shore.

Keeping wet
To stop drying up, common limpets (2) cling so firmly to the rocks when the tide is out, that their shells cut a groove in the stone. They always return to the same spot on a rock.

The bladder wrack (1) and serrated wrack (4) can survive out of water for several hours. The sea-oak (33), sea-lettuce (22) and peacock's tail (21), however, will quickly dry up and die out of water, so they always live in pools or shallow water.

The common blenny (16) eats barnacles and mussels. It has a smooth body and can slither short distances through weeds and over rocks from one pool to another. The two slug-like sea-lemons (23) are feeding on the breadcrumb sponge (24).

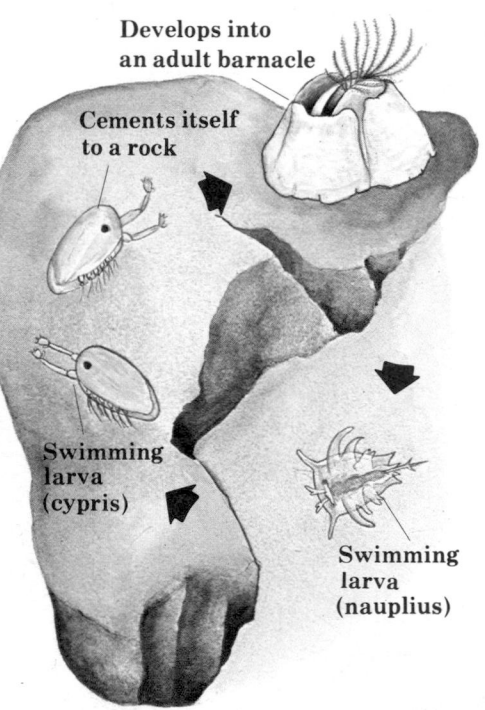

Develops into
an adult barnacle

Cements itself
to a rock

Swimming
larva
(cypris)

Swimming
larva
(nauplius)

▲ Barnacle life cycle
The eggs hatch into tiny swimming larvae (1). Each larva grows extra segments, eyes and mouthparts. After three weeks it changes into a two-shelled larva (2) and looks for a home. It cements itself on to a rock (3) and grows into an adult barnacle (4).

▼ Dogwhelks
Dogwhelks are carnivores. They have long drill-like mouthparts, with which they bore holes in the shells of mussels or barnacles, and suck out the contents. Dirty-white dogwhelks have eaten only barnacles (1). Those that only eat mussels are darker (2). Stripey dogwhelks have had a mixed diet (3).

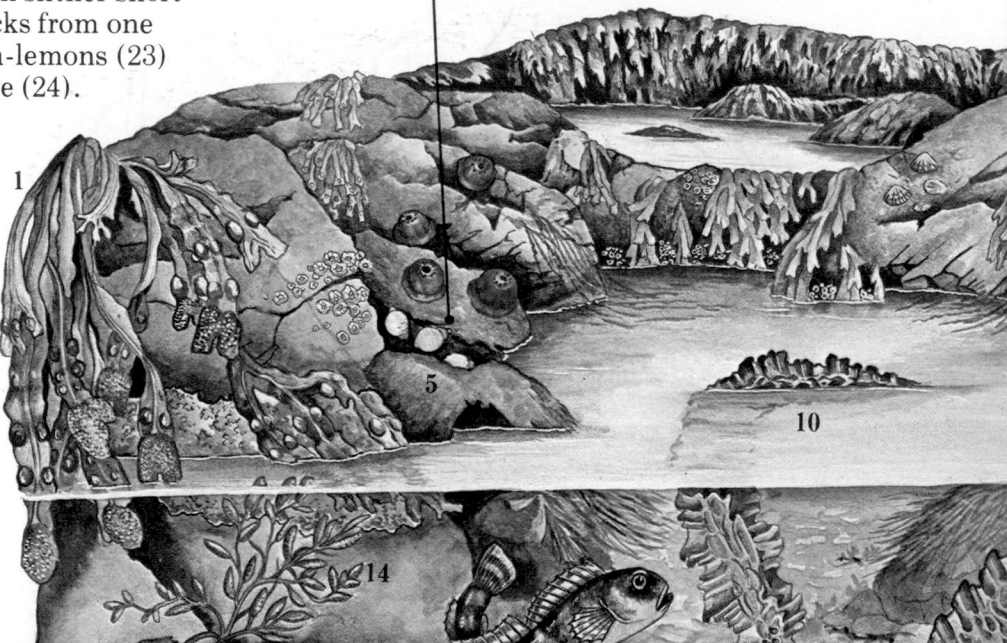

Key	10 Sea-belt	22 Sea-lettuce
	11 Prawn	23 Sea-lemon
1 Bladder wrack	12 Cystoseira	24 Breadcrumb sponge
2 Limpets	13 Brittle-star	25 Common starfish
3 Periwinkles	14 Pod weed	26 Green sea-urchin
4 Serrated wrack	15 Shore crab	27 Oyster
5 Dogwhelks	16 Blenny	28 Cushion star
6 Barnacles	17 Chiton	29 Hermit crab
7 Enteromorpha	18 Topshells	30 Hermit crab anemone
8 Springtails	19 Snakelocks anemone	31 Pea crab
9 Mussels	20 Beadlet anemone	32 Coral weed
	21 Peacock's tail	33 Sea oak

Feeding habits

The tentacles of the snakelocks anemone (19) wave gently in the water. If the small prawn (11) touches them, it will be paralysed. The tentacles will then guide the food into the anemone's mouth, in the middle of the tentacles.

The hermit crab anemone (30) lives on the hermit crab's whelk shell (29). The anemone helps to disguise the crab. In return it eats food scraps left by the crab.

The barnacles (6) are busy feeding. Their six feathery legs kick in and out, straining tiny particles of food from the water.

◀ Life on a holdfast

Many seaweeds are attached to rocks by leathery, root-like structures called **holdfasts.**

Several animals live in this oarweed holdfast. It shelters them against waves, hides them from enemies and stops them from drying up.

◀ Key	4 Blue-rayed limpet
1 Stalked jellyfish	5 Shore crab
2 Beadlet anemone	6 Mussels
3 Sea squirt	7 Keelworms

▼ Springtails

The springtail is one of the few insects found on the beach. Look for it on the surface of sea-water trapped in small, rocky hollows. Large groups of them float round and round, looking like patches of blue-black velvet.

▼ Pea crab

The tiny, almost transparent pea crab lives inside the shells of living molluscs, such as mussels, oysters and cockles. The crab keeps the mollusc clean by eating scraps of food from its gills.

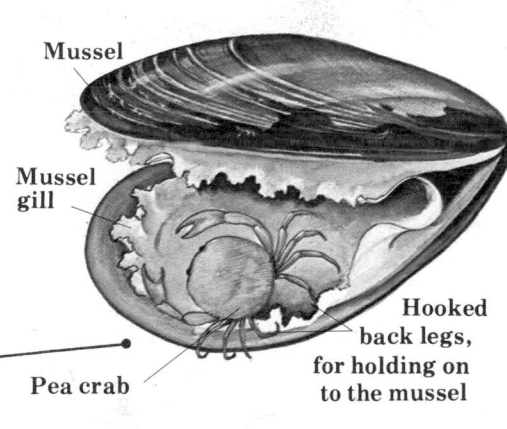

Mussel

Mussel gill

Pea crab

Hooked back legs, for holding on to the mussel

Molluscs

Molluscs are mostly small, slow-moving animals with gills and a chalky shell. They are found everywhere on the shore, at different levels, depending on how long they can live out of water, uncovered by the tide.

Some are like the slugs and snails that live on land. Others, called bivalves, have two hinged shells. They burrow in mud and sand, and sometimes in wood and rock. The octopus is a mollusc, although its shell is inside its body.

* Not to scale. The average length of body is given.

How a razor shell burrows

1 The muscular foot wriggles into the sand. It is hatchet-shaped, so that it cannot easily be pulled out of the sand.
2 The foot contracts, pulling the shell upright.
3 The foot wriggles deeper into the sand. When it contracts again, the shell is pulled further down.
4 The razor shell can bury itself very quickly. Water, containing food and oxygen, is taken to and from the body through special tubes called siphons.

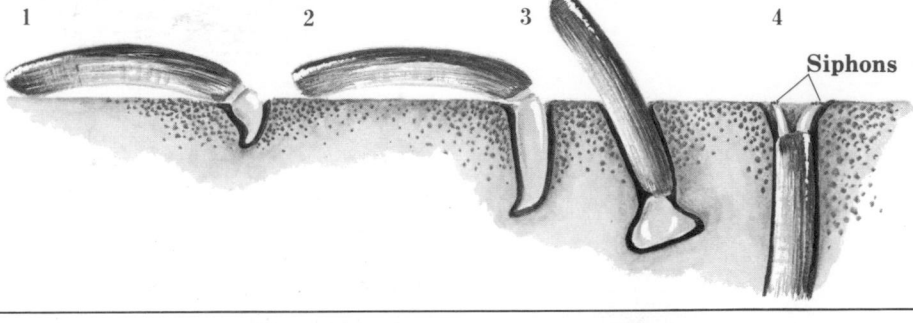

Siphons

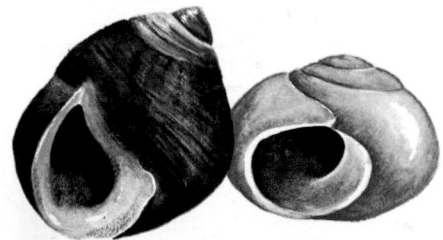

▲**Periwinkles: Edible** 2.5cm high (left) **Flat** 1cm high (right)
There are several different kinds of these common, snail-like molluscs. Each is found at a different level on the shore. They feed on seaweed and vary in colour.

▲**Topshells: Painted** 2.5cm high (left) **Grey** 1.25cm high (right)
These are the two most common topshells. The grey topshell is flatter and less brightly coloured than the painted topshell, and is very common.

▲**Cockle** 5cm (left) **Tellin** 2cm (right)
These bivalves burrow in sand and mud in the middle and lower shore. With its long siphons, the cockle sifts food from the sand. The tellin sucks food from the surface of the sand.

▲**Common limpet** 7cm
Limpets are snails with cone-shaped shells, and are found on rocky shores. They feed on seaweeds, using a rasping tongue. They stick firmly to a rock when the tide goes out, and trap water inside their shells.

▲ **Blue-rayed limpet** 2cm
This beautiful animal lives on oarweeds. It is common on rocky beaches, usually in the lower shore zone. Its shell is smooth, and almost transparent, with several rows of bright blue spots. These become duller with age.

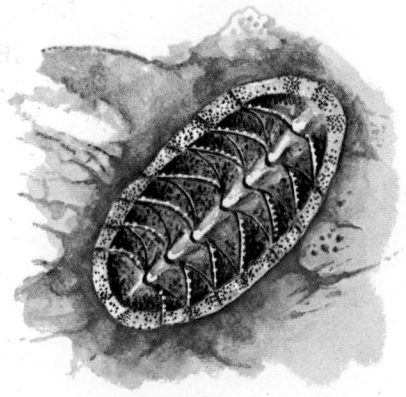

▲**Chiton** 2cm
The shell of this small, shield-shaped mollusc is made up of eight overlapping plates. It is sometimes called a 'coat-of-mail' shell and can curl up, like a woodlouse. Small numbers of chitons can be found under rocks.

▲ Queen scallop 9cm
An edible bivalve which lives offshore, usually on sand. It can swim away from danger, such as a starfish, by clapping its shells together. Single shells are often washed up by the tide.

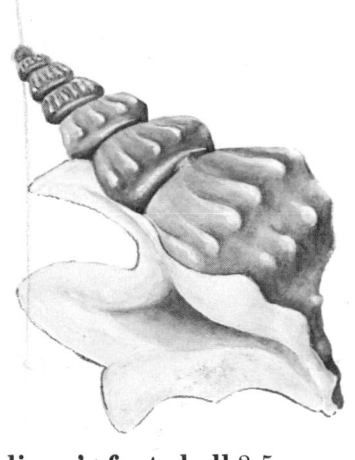

▲ Pelican's foot shell 3.5cm
You may find this unusual shell washed up on the beach. When alive it lives in deep water, where it burrows in mud and sand. Its name comes from the 'wing' on the shell, which looks like a pelican's foot.

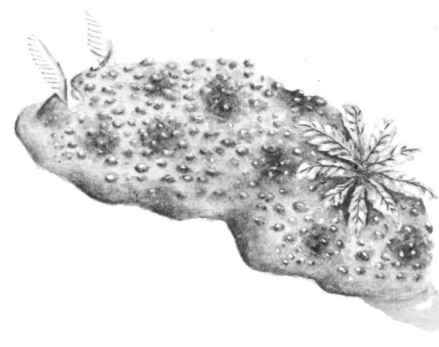

▲ Sea-lemon 7cm
This slug-like mollusc has no shell. Its yellowish body looks rather like a piece of lemon peel. In summer it is sometimes found in rocky pools on the lower shore. Look for the flower-like gills on its back.

▲ Common mussel 1-10cm
This very common bivalve attaches itself to rocks by strong 'byssus' threads. It lives on rocky shores, or on stones on muddy shores. You will often find clusters of small mussels in rocky crevices.

▲ Common whelk 8cm high
The common or edible whelk lives in the sea, where it feeds on seaweeds and other molluscs, such as mussels. Empty whelk shells are washed ashore, and often become homes for hermit crabs.

▲ Dogwhelk 3cm high
Dogwhelks are smaller than common whelks. They are also carnivores, and eat mussels and barnacles, using a rasping tongue. The colour of dogwhelks depends on their diet. They live on the middle shore.

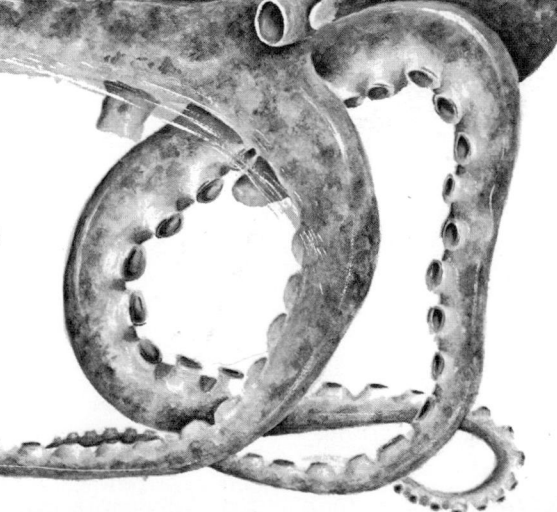

▲ Portuguese oyster 15cm wide
This oyster came originally from the Bay of Biscay and was grown in oyster beds for food. It now also lives in estuaries attached to small stones and shells. Amazingly, it is male one year and female the next!

▶ Lesser octopus up to 50cm
An uncommon mollusc, with eight arms, each with a row of suckers. It lurks among rocks on the lowest part of the shore. It has well developed eyes and can change colour to match its background.

The crab family

Crabs, shrimps, prawns and lobsters are all crustaceans. They are relatives of the insects and spiders, and have many jointed legs. They usually have a heavy, hard outer skeleton, which makes many crustaceans slow movers. They come in all shapes and sizes, and nearly all live in or near water.

* Not to scale. The average length is given.

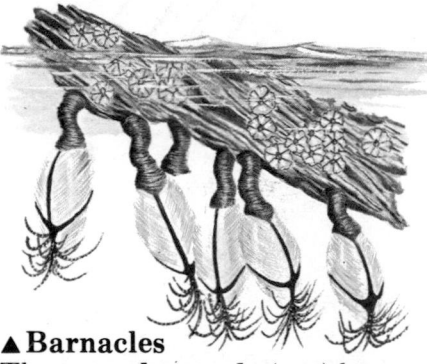

▲ **Barnacles**
The **goose barnacle** (top) has a long stalk. It lives on floating objects, or on rocks and piers.
▼ **Acorn** and **star barnacles** live everywhere on rocks, wood and even other shelled animals. When the tide is out the tiny animal hides inside the hard chalky plates. Water and air are trapped inside. When the tide returns six pairs of feathery legs beat in and out, trapping food.

Acorn barnacle (left): has a diamond-shaped opening, and is found all over the shore.

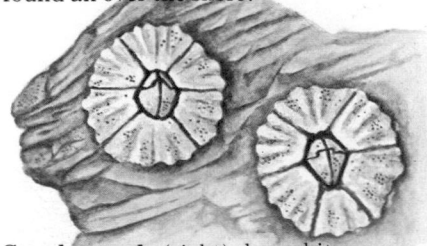

Star barnacle (right): has a kite-shaped opening, and lives in middle and upper shore zones.

▲ **Common shore crab** 10cm
Very common on the middle and lower parts of most shores, hiding under seaweeds and stones. It can live out of water for quite a long time. It feeds on sandhoppers, molluscs and animal remains.

▲ **Velvet swimming crab** 5-10cm
A beautiful, but very fierce, lower-shore crab. The last part of the back legs is flat, and is used as a paddle when swimming. Look for the hairy shell, and for the blue marks on its legs and pincers.

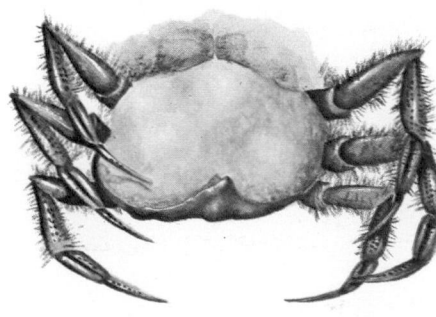

▲ **Parasitic barnacle**
This strange animal lives under the abdomen of shore crabs. It looks like a large yellow leathery sac. These are its reproductive parts. The actual barnacle is underneath, living on the crab's body.

▲ **Edible crab** 5-25cm
You may find this common crab on the middle and lower parts of the shore, under stones and seaweed. Look for the 'piecrust' edge to its pinky-brown shell. It can be cooked and eaten.

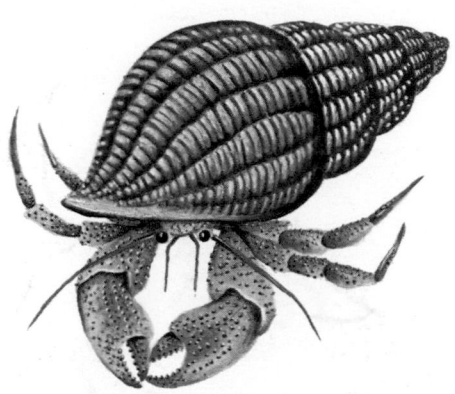

▲ **Common hermit crab** 10cm
Hermit crabs have soft abdomens, so they protect themselves by living in the empty shells of winkles, topshells and whelks. When they have outgrown one shell they find a larger one.

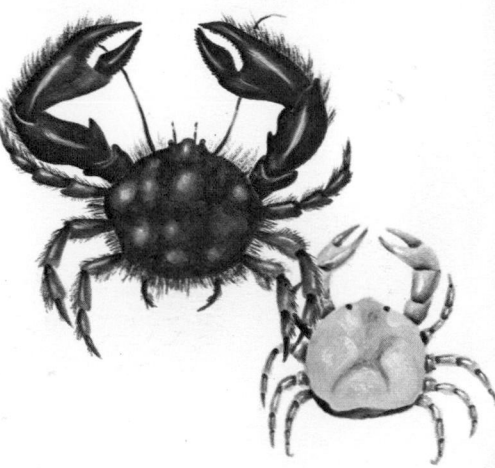

▲ **Broad-clawed porcelain crab** 1.2cm (left)
This is not a true crab. It is common under stones and in mud.

▲ **Pea crab** 1.5cm (right)
Lives inside the shells of living oysters and mussels.

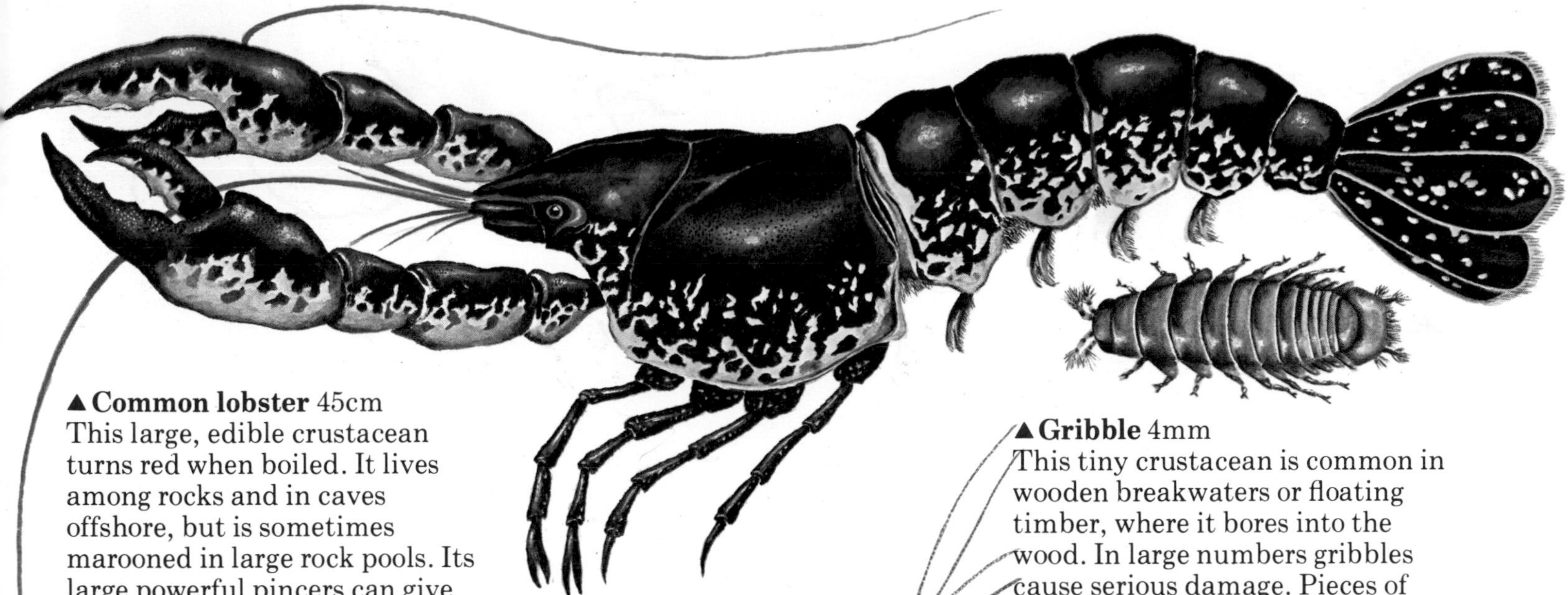

▲ Common lobster 45cm
This large, edible crustacean turns red when boiled. It lives among rocks and in caves offshore, but is sometimes marooned in large rock pools. Its large powerful pincers can give you a nasty nip.

▲ Gribble 4mm
This tiny crustacean is common in wooden breakwaters or floating timber, where it bores into the wood. In large numbers gribbles cause serious damage. Pieces of gribble-bored wood are often washed up on beaches.

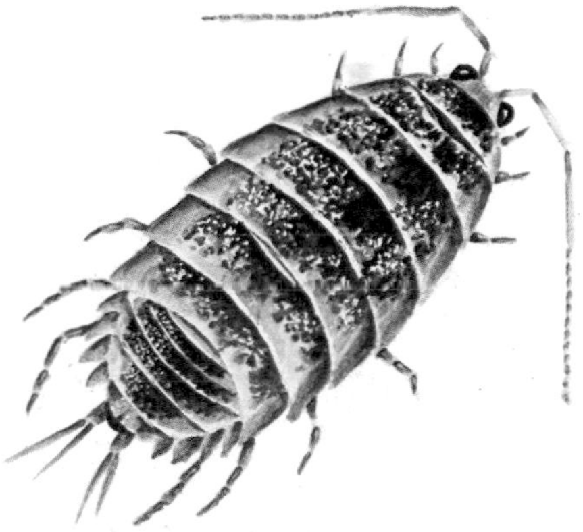

▲ Common shrimp 5cm
Shrimps live in sandy shore pools, shallow water and estuaries, usually in large numbers. They are not transparent, like prawns. They burrow in the sand, and feed on ragworms and small crustaceans.

▲ Common prawn 5-10cm
Prawns are very common in rocky and sandy pools on the middle and lower shore. They hide under weed, and their almost transparent bodies are difficult to spot as they dart about. This species is edible.

▲ Sea slater 2cm
A common splash-zone crustacean which lives under stones and weeds. It is also common in cracks in harbour walls. It hides during the day, only coming out at night to feed on brown seaweeds.

▲ Sandhopper 1.5cm
Found in large numbers on the upper shore, where they burrow in the sand and amongst their food: rotting seaweed and dead animal remains. When disturbed, they leap in all directions. They cannot live underwater for very long.

How a prawn moults

Crustaceans, like this prawn, are supported by a stiff outer shell, not an internal skeleton. The shell does not grow, so as the animal grows it has to shed its shell. This is called *moulting*. The shell splits, and the animal wriggles out (left). A soft, larger shell has already developed. This slowly hardens. The animal hides until its new shell is hard.

Sand dunes

Sand is a difficult habitat to live in. It quickly dries out and is blown about by the wind, so only the toughest plants can survive. Dunes are formed when sand piles up round objects, usually plants.

Dunes near the beach

Only really tough plants like sea sandwort (36) can grow at the top of the beach. Their thick, fleshy leaves store fresh water and long roots anchor them firmly in the shifting sand.

If an object like a picnic box is left on a windy beach a heap of dry sand will build up around it and soon cover it up. This is how dunes are formed. The long creeping roots of sand couch (31), marram grass (30) and sea lyme-grass (28) bind the sand together. Windblown sand builds up around the plants forming small dunes.

▼Sand couch

Sand couch lives almost on the beach, and is sometimes covered by the tide. It has spreading underground stems which help to bind the sand together. New shoots sprout on the stems and push up through the sand.

▶ Marram grass

The sand dunes are very dry unless it rains. Marram grass cuts down water loss from its leaves by rolling them up into a tube (1). The outside of this leafy tube is quite waterproof. If it rains the leaf will unroll (2).

Cream and brown **banded snails** are common on sand dunes.

Yellow dunes

Marram grass can grow up through the sand and has long underground roots. Because it lives further from the sea than sand couch, dunes become higher as you move inland. Colonies of common terns (13) may nest here.

Many more plants grow on the sheltered side away from the sea. Sand fescue grass also helps to bind the sand together. You may see sea holly (33), sea campion (21), prickly saltwort (27), sea bindweed (32) and sea rocket (29).

As more plants grow and die, a richer, grey soil is formed.

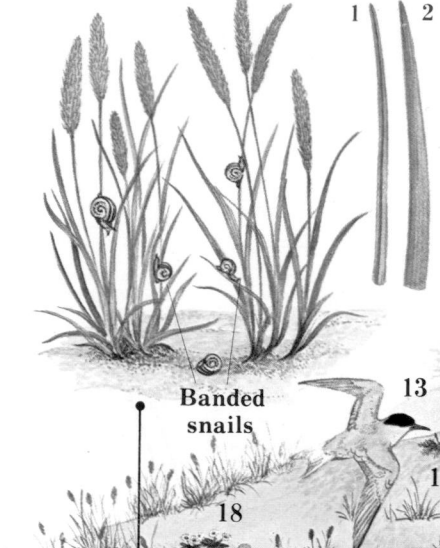

Banded snails

Aerial shoot

Roots　　Underground stem

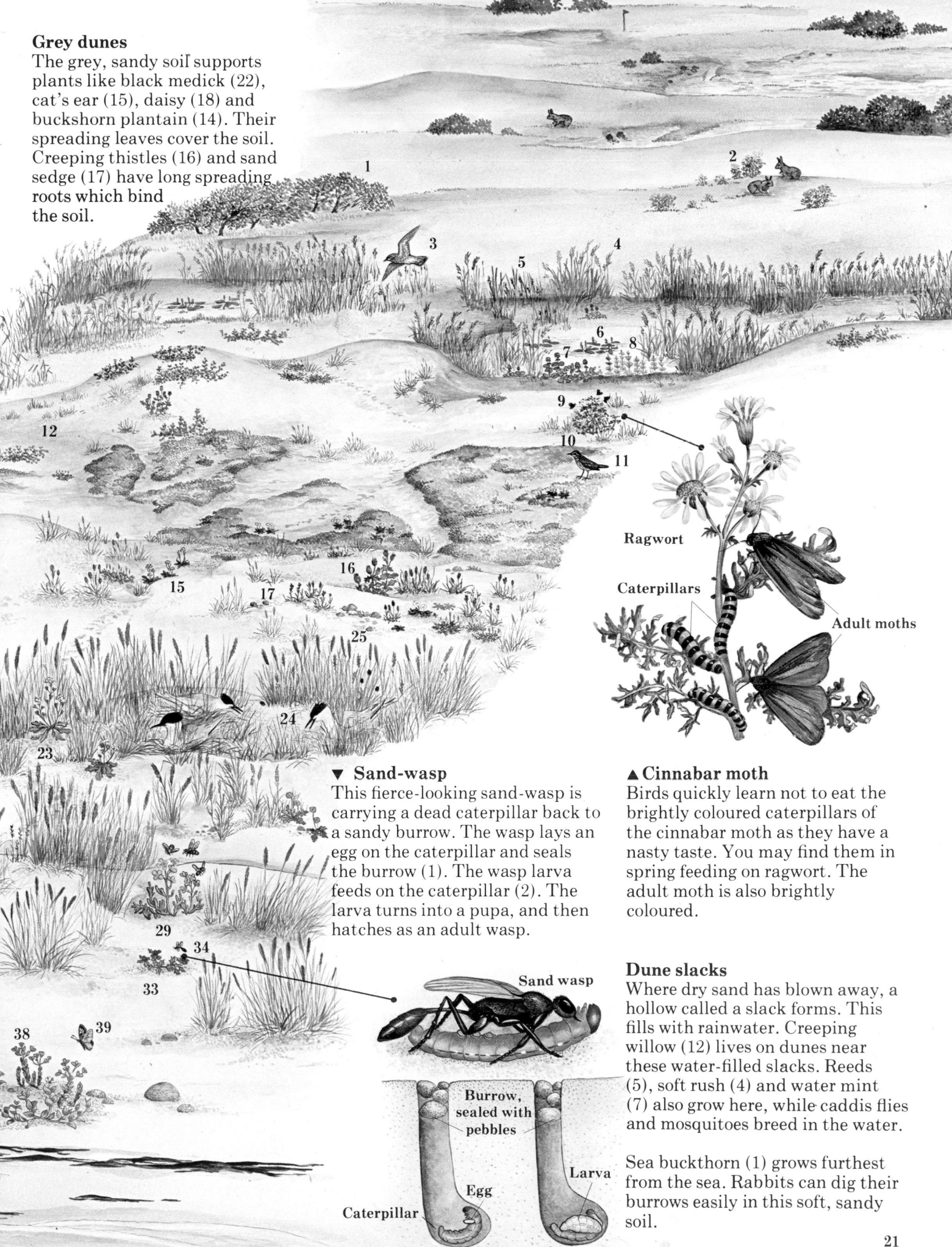

Grey dunes
The grey, sandy soil supports plants like black medick (22), cat's ear (15), daisy (18) and buckshorn plantain (14). Their spreading leaves cover the soil. Creeping thistles (16) and sand sedge (17) have long spreading roots which bind the soil.

Ragwort

Caterpillars

Adult moths

▼ Sand-wasp
This fierce-looking sand-wasp is carrying a dead caterpillar back to a sandy burrow. The wasp lays an egg on the caterpillar and seals the burrow (1). The wasp larva feeds on the caterpillar (2). The larva turns into a pupa, and then hatches as an adult wasp.

▲ Cinnabar moth
Birds quickly learn not to eat the brightly coloured caterpillars of the cinnabar moth as they have a nasty taste. You may find them in spring feeding on ragwort. The adult moth is also brightly coloured.

Dune slacks
Where dry sand has blown away, a hollow called a slack forms. This fills with rainwater. Creeping willow (12) lives on dunes near these water-filled slacks. Reeds (5), soft rush (4) and water mint (7) also grow here, while caddis flies and mosquitoes breed in the water.

Sea buckthorn (1) grows furthest from the sea. Rabbits can dig their burrows easily in this soft, sandy soil.

Sand wasp

Burrow, sealed with pebbles

Larva

Egg

Caterpillar

1

2

Beach plants

There are two main groups of plants on the beach. The plants that are covered by the sea are nearly all algae, and are more commonly known as seaweeds. They have no flowers. Above the tide-line, a few tough flowering plants are found. Many have roots which grow deep into the sand and mud.

* Not to scale. The average height is given.

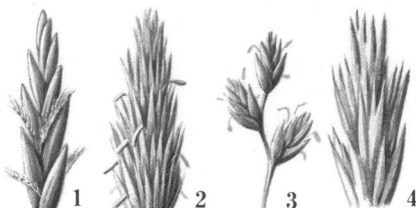

▲**Sea sandwort** 20cm
Common on shingle and sandy beaches, where the creeping stems and forked branches often cover quite large areas. The carpet of small fleshy leaves and the spreading roots help to bind the sand together.

▲**Prickly saltwort** 60cm
An upright or spreading plant found on salt-marshes and sandy beaches. The thick, tough stem has pink or green stripes, and many branches. There are tough prickles at the tips of the fleshy leaves.

▲ **Yellow horned-poppy** 60-80cm
Found growing on sand dunes, shingle and chalky cliffs. In summer, look for the lovely golden yellow flowers up to 8cm across. The seed pods, like curved horns, may be 30cm long. Poisonous.

▲ **Sea rocket** 20-40cm
A straggling, untidy-looking plant with zigzag branches and thick fleshy leaves. It grows near the high-tide mark on sandy beaches and salt-marshes. Clusters of pale mauve flowers appear in summer.

▲ **Sea holly** 50cm
This prickly plant grows on sandy and shingle beaches, in and above the splash zone. The bluish-green, holly-like leaves have white edges. The pale blue flowerheads are also prickly.

▲ **Samphire** 30cm
Sometimes found growing in rocky crevices on the upper shore. The stem and leaves are thick and fleshy, containing water. The leaves are sometimes picked in spring and pickled, like onions.

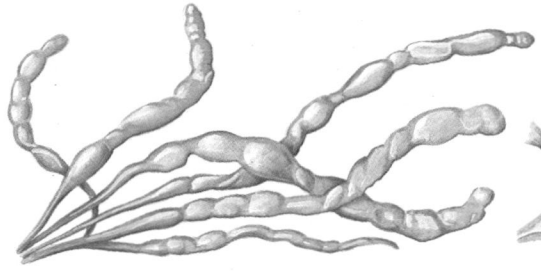

▲ Enteromorpha 5-80cm
A very common seaweed, found in most upper shore pools, attached to stones and shells. Its crinkly green fronds are hollow and up to 80cm long. They fill with gas as they grow, and float if broken off.

▲ Sea-lettuce 15–50cm
The large, almost transparent fronds look a bit like lettuce leaves. It is very common on the middle and lower shore and in pools on the upper shore, attached to stones and shells.

▲ Thong weed Body 5cm, strap up to 200cm
Look for olive-brown, mushroom-like plants on the lower shore. Several long, branched, leathery 'straps' will grow from the dent in the top of each one.

▲ Lomentaria 15cm (right)
Lomentaria looks like strings of tiny pink sausages.

▲ Coral weed 8cm (left)
The tiny stiff fronds of coral weed have a hard 'skeleton' of lime, like coral.

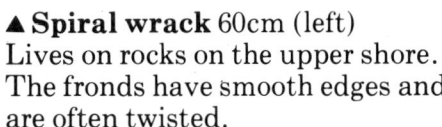

▲ Spiral wrack 60cm (left)
Lives on rocks on the upper shore. The fronds have smooth edges and are often twisted.

▲ Serrated wrack 60cm (right)
Lives on the lower shore. It is easy to spot by the toothed, saw-like edge to the fronds.

▶ Bladder wrack 15-100cm
Very common on the middle shore. The leathery, strap-like fronds have wavy edges, and many pairs of air-filled bladders.

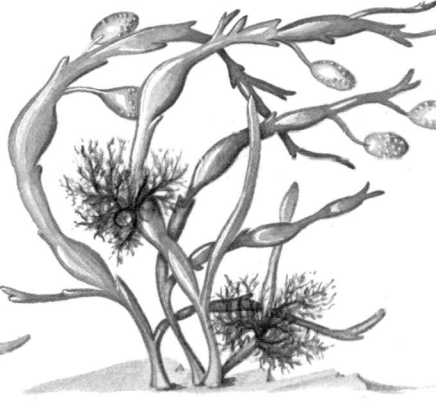

▲ Egg wrack 30-150cm
Very common on sheltered beaches and in estuaries, attached to rocks on the middle shore. The long straggly fronds have air-filled bladders. A small, red, tufted seaweed often grows on egg wrack.

▲ Irish moss 7-15cm
A very common seaweed, found on middle and lower parts of rocky shores. Its colour varies from light green to dark red. It has many branches, which make it look rounded. It is also called **carragheen.**

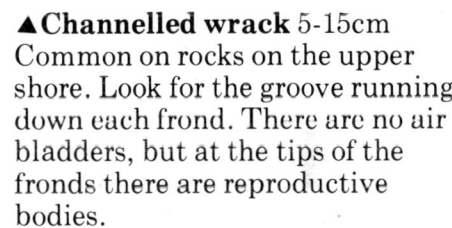

▲ Channelled wrack 5-15cm
Common on rocks on the upper shore. Look for the groove running down each frond. There are no air bladders, but at the tips of the fronds there are reproductive bodies.

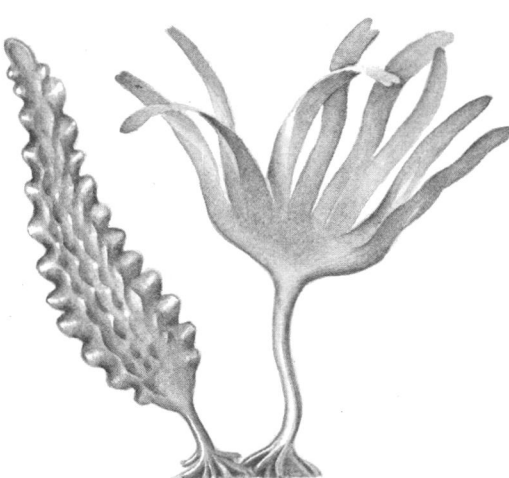

▲ Oarweed Up to 300cm
Oarweeds grow low on the shore and are rarely uncovered by the tide. Small plants grow in rock pools. One kind, called sea-belt (left), has long fronds.
Another, divided into 'fingers', is called tangleweed (right).

Shore birds

Many different kinds of birds live and feed on the shore. As well as seagulls, there is a large group of birds called waders. They run around at the water's edge, probing the sand or mud for food. Waders are often seen in huge flocks in winter.

* Not to scale. Average body length given.

Birds which feed in mud

The beaks of wading birds are different lengths, so each species feeds on different mud-living animals. For example, **knots** have very short beaks. They feed on animals which live near the surface, like crabs, worms and small molluscs. **Curlews** have very long beaks, which go far into the mud. They can reach deep-burrowing lugworms, ragworms and bivalve molluscs.

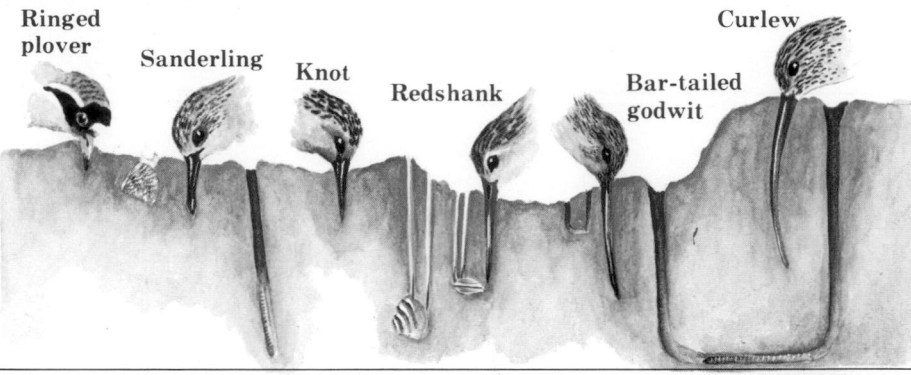

Ringed plover   Sanderling   Knot   Redshank   Bar-tailed godwit   Curlew

▲ **Black-headed gull** 38cm
One of the most common birds on shores, mudflats and estuaries, often in noisy flocks. They breed in colonies on shingle banks, moors and lakes. In summer the head is chocolate brown (not black).

▲ **Curlew** 58cm
The largest European wading bird. It is very shy, with a sad call (coor-lee: coor-lee). Curlews are common on mudflats and estuaries. They nest on moors, marshes, meadows and sand-dunes.

▲ **Oystercatcher** 43cm
A very noisy bird, with a 'kleep-kleep' call. It is easy to recognize, with its black upper parts, white underparts and orange beak. It eats oysters, mussels, limpets, crustaceans and worms.

▲ **Ringed plover** 19cm
A small, plump bird, which runs about near the sea, often pausing to search for food. Look for its orange legs and the wide black band across its chest. Large flocks live on sandy and muddy shores.

▲ **Turnstone** 23cm
The speckled feathers help to camouflage the turnstone on stony and muddy beaches. It turns over stones, shells and rubbish with its beak as it searches for food, like mussels, limpets and sandhoppers.

▲ **Sanderling** 20cm
Another small, plump, very active wader. When looking for food it races up and down the tideline like a clockwork toy. It spends the winter on sandy beaches, and breeds on stony ground in the Arctic.

Dunlin 18cm

Possibly the most common wader, found in huge flocks on estuaries, mudflats, salt-marshes and sandy beaches. In summer it is the only small wader with a black belly. When feeding it looks hunched up.

Bar-tailed godwit 38cm

This large wader looks like a curlew, but its long beak curves slightly upwards. It gets its name from the stripe of brownish-grey feathers on its white tail. It is very common on estuaries and mudflats.

Summer plumage

Knot 25cm

Huge flocks of knots can often be seen searching for molluscs and worms on sandy and muddy shores. They all face in the same direction. If disturbed, the flock will take off like a grey cloud.

▶ Redshank 28cm

A noisy, restless wader, which springs into the air at the slightest sign of danger. It gets its name from the colour of its legs. It is a common shore bird, and nests in grassland and marshy places near the sea.

▲ Common tern 35cm

In summer the common tern's beak becomes orange-red with a black tip. You may see terns hovering above the sea looking for fish. They nest in sand dunes and beaches.

▲ Little tern 24cm

A very small tern with a black-tipped yellow beak. They tend to hover longer than common terns before diving. They nest in small colonies on sandy and shingly beaches and, in Europe, beside lakes and rivers.

▲ Shelduck 61cm

A large, goose-like duck, which lives on mudflats, estuaries and sandy coasts, and feeds on snails. It sometimes nests in rabbit burrows. You can recognize the male by the knob on its beak.

▲ Avocet 43cm

A large, rare wader with an unmistakable beak. It lives on mudflats, estuaries and sand banks. It feeds in shallow water, sifting it with a side-to-side movement of the beak.

Cliffs

The kinds of plants and animals found on cliffs depends on the type of rocks and the amount of soil. Smooth rocks and narrow ledges exposed to hot sun, rain and salt spray are unfriendly places to make a home.

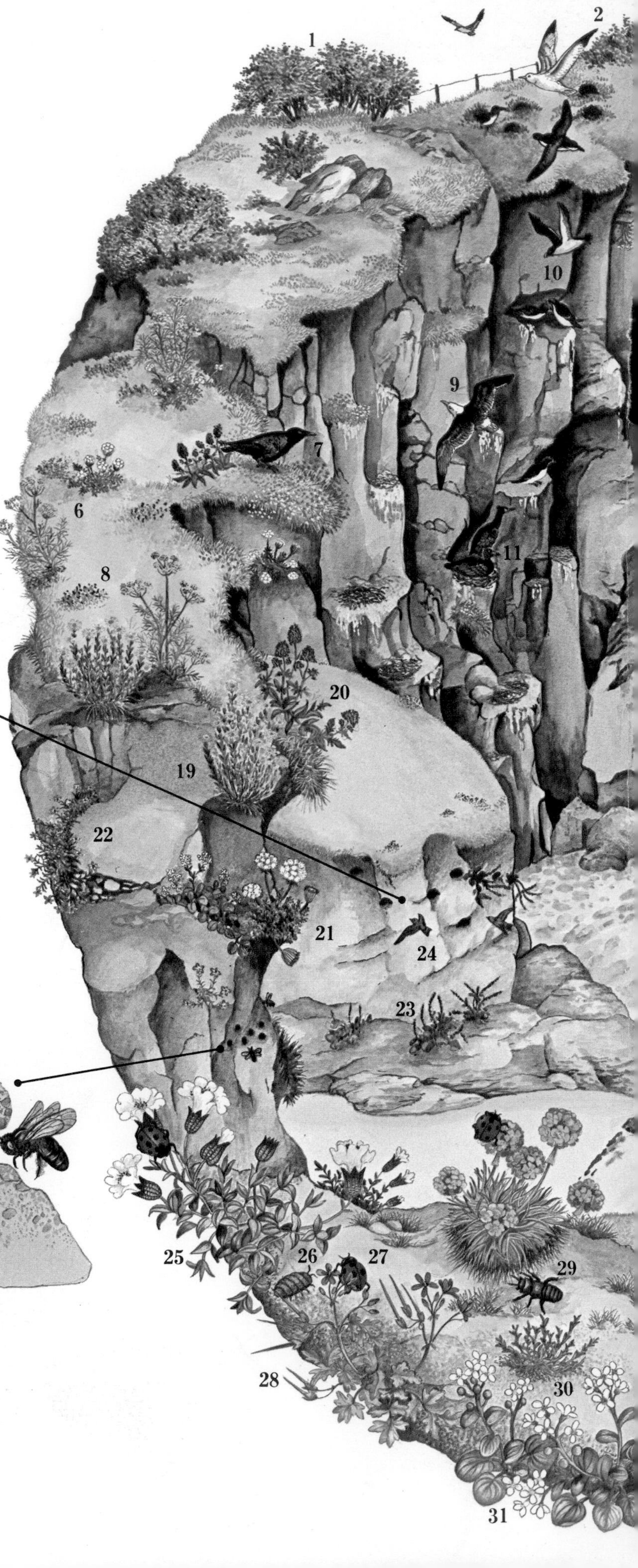

Birds

Birds are the only animals that can reach the cliff ledges easily. Here, noisy colonies of herring gulls (33), razorbills (10) and guillemots (17) will make their nests. The Manx shearwater (5) nests in burrows in the soil on top of the cliff.

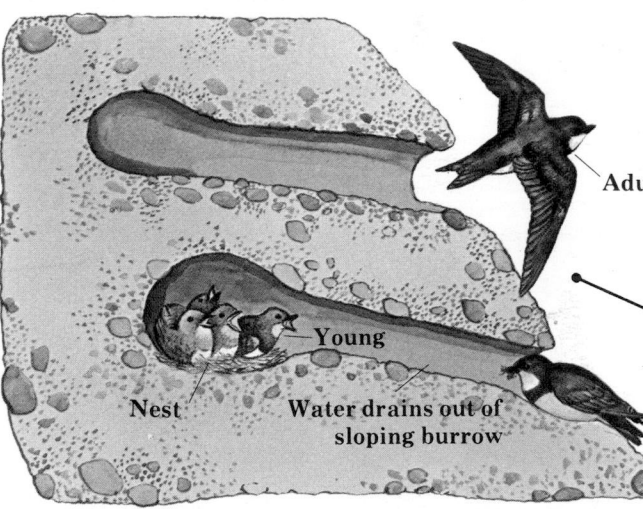

▲ Sand martins

The sand martin nests in colonies in sand and gravel cliffs. Both parents dig a burrow about 1 metre long, and make a nest at the end. The young are fed on insects caught by the parents as they fly. The burrows may be used for several years until they become too full of fleas.

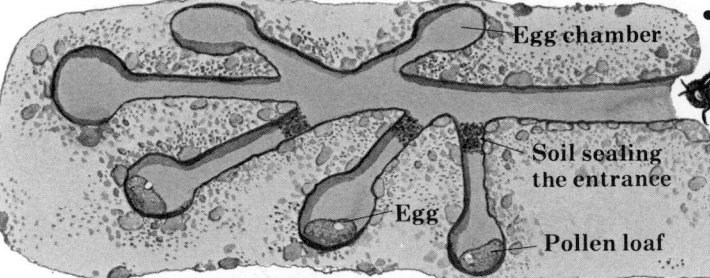

▲ Solitary bees

These insects live in small holes in sandy cliffs. The female digs a burrow in spring. In each chamber, she lays an egg on a tiny loaf of pollen. The larva grows as it eats the pollen. It turns into a pupa and an adult hatches in the summer. The young bees mate and lay eggs. New adults emerge next spring.

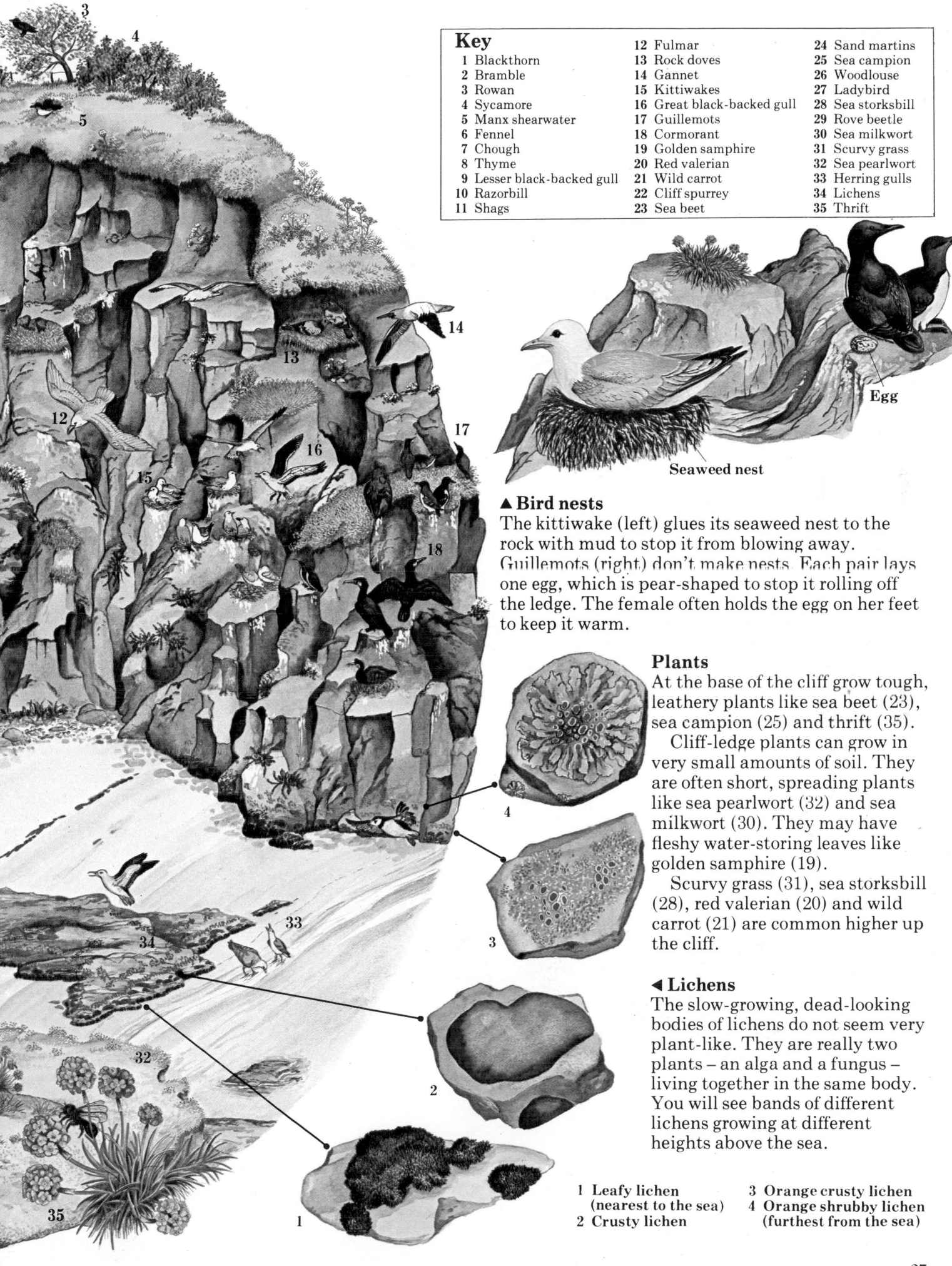

Key

1 Blackthorn
2 Bramble
3 Rowan
4 Sycamore
5 Manx shearwater
6 Fennel
7 Chough
8 Thyme
9 Lesser black-backed gull
10 Razorbill
11 Shags

12 Fulmar
13 Rock doves
14 Gannet
15 Kittiwakes
16 Great black-backed gull
17 Guillemots
18 Cormorant
19 Golden samphire
20 Red valerian
21 Wild carrot
22 Cliff spurrey
23 Sea beet

24 Sand martins
25 Sea campion
26 Woodlouse
27 Ladybird
28 Sea storksbill
29 Rove beetle
30 Sea milkwort
31 Scurvy grass
32 Sea pearlwort
33 Herring gulls
34 Lichens
35 Thrift

Egg

Seaweed nest

▲ Bird nests

The kittiwake (left) glues its seaweed nest to the rock with mud to stop it from blowing away. Guillemots (right) don't make nests. Each pair lays one egg, which is pear-shaped to stop it rolling off the ledge. The female often holds the egg on her feet to keep it warm.

Plants

At the base of the cliff grow tough, leathery plants like sea beet (23), sea campion (25) and thrift (35).

Cliff-ledge plants can grow in very small amounts of soil. They are often short, spreading plants like sea pearlwort (32) and sea milkwort (30). They may have fleshy water-storing leaves like golden samphire (19).

Scurvy grass (31), sea storksbill (28), red valerian (20) and wild carrot (21) are common higher up the cliff.

◀ Lichens

The slow-growing, dead-looking bodies of lichens do not seem very plant-like. They are really two plants – an alga and a fungus – living together in the same body. You will see bands of different lichens growing at different heights above the sea.

1 **Leafy lichen**
(nearest to the sea)
2 **Crusty lichen**

3 **Orange crusty lichen**
4 **Orange shrubby lichen**
(furthest from the sea)

Cliff birds

Many seabirds and some inland birds use sheltered cracks and caves in rocks near the sea for roosting and nesting. During the summer breeding season enormous numbers of seabirds will colonize a particular cliff or rocky island.

Some birds nest in burrows in the cliff soil. They may dig their own or use old rabbit warrens.

* Not to scale. Average body length given.

▲ **Cormorant** 91cm
A sleek bird often seen perched on a rock or post with its wings outstretched to dry. It swims low in the water and dives for fish. Notice its hooked beak. Cormorants nest in groups on rocky ledges.

▲ **Puffin** 30cm
The colourful, grooved, parrot-like beak is smaller in winter as the outer layer is shed. Puffins swim and dive very well. They nest in rabbit holes or dig burrows in turf on cliffs on grassy islands.

▲ **Razorbill** 40cm
Look for the flat axe-shaped beak with white lines. Large colonies perch and nest on rocky ledges, often with puffins and guillemots. Like penguins they walk upright and are excellent swimmers.

▲ **Guillemot** 42cm
Guillemots look like razorbills but have slender pointed beaks and thinner necks. They live in enormous, noisy colonies on open cliff ledges. When flying, their wings make a whirring sound.

◀ **Rock dove** 33cm
This is the ancestor of the domestic pigeon seen in towns, and makes the same 'oo-roo-coo' noise. It lives on rocky sea cliffs, where it nests in rocky crevices and caves, and eats seeds.

▲ **Manx shearwater** 36cm
During the breeding season this bird can often be seen gliding low over the waves or swimming in large flocks. As it flies, its wings show alternately black and white. It nests in burrows on cliffs.

▲ Kittiwake 40cm
A gull which lives on the open sea except in the breeding season. It nests on steep cliffs or in caves. It swims and dives for fish and crustaceans. It gets its name from its call 'kitti-wa-ak'.

Young herring gulls

When gulls hatch, they look completely different from their parents. They are mottled brown, with brown beaks. After a year they are fully grown, but still have brown feathers and beaks. It takes another year for the adult feathers to grow. It is very difficult to tell the young of one gull from another.

Young gull

Adult herring gull

Chicks

▲ Herring gull 56cm
The most common coastal gull, with paler upper parts than the lesser black-backed gull. It eats worms, which it digs up, and breaks open molluscs by dropping them from a height on to stones.

▲ Great black-backed gull 68cm
This large, strong-winged gull steals from other birds. It robs nests, eating the eggs and young, and may kill other birds for food. Notice the pink legs and the massive yellow beak with a red spot.

▲ Lesser black-backed gull 53cm
Smaller birds than great black-backed gulls, with paler backs and wings. They live in colonies, usually on cliffs. As well as eating crabs and molluscs they take eggs from nests and eat rotting fish.

▲ Storm petrel 15cm
The smallest European seabird, once called 'Mother Carey's chicken' by sailors. If they saw one they expected storms. As it skims over the waves it looks as if it is treading on the water with its webbed feet.

▶ Gannet 91cm
This is a large bird which lives on the open sea. It catches fish by plunging into the sea with its wings folded back from as much as 30m. It breeds in a few enormous colonies on cliffs in the North Atlantic.

Coastal plants

Many plants only grow near the sea. They prefer the salty air and soil. Some of them are varieties of inland plants.

Many coastal plants have fleshy leaves, which contain stores of fresh water. These emergency stores can be used when rainwater is in short supply.

* Not to scale. The average height is given.

▲ Sea lavender 15-30cm
A common plant on salt-marshes and mudflats. It is not related to garden lavender, though its flowers are the same colour. It flowers in summer and autumn, often forming a purple carpet.

▲ Wall pepper 8cm
The tiny, fleshy, green leaves have a bitter, peppery taste, which gives the plant its name. It is common on shingle beaches and sand dunes. Look for the trailing stems and golden yellow flowers.

▲Sea plantain 15cm
Commonly found on cliffs and salt-marshes. Most of the leaves are long and fleshy and may be up to 30cm long. Other leaves are short and thin, like blades of grass. Spiky flowers appear in summer.

▲ Danish scurvy grass 20cm
This common plant is not a grass. It grows on damp sea cliffs and muddy seashore banks. Long ago sailors used to eat its heart-shaped leaves, which are rich in Vitamin C. This helped to cure a disease called scurvy.

▲ Sea purslane 40-60cm
A salt-marsh plant, which is also found on mudflats and sandy shores. Look for the thick, fleshy, spoon-shaped leaves and the tiny yellow-green flowers. The stems and leaves have a mealy white coating.

▲ Golden samphire 40-60cm
Found on salt-marshes, seawalls and among rocks on cliffs. The golden yellow flowers appear in late summer. The upright stem bears many small, thick, fleshy leaves, some with three points at the tip.

▲ Sea campion 15-20cm
Lives on firm shingle beaches, sandy shores and cliff ledges. It can grow in very little soil. On shingle, the plants cling to the surface, forming a mat. In summer it has white flowers, which are unmistakable.

▲ Sea spurge 20-30cm
A common plant on sandy shores. The greenish-grey, leathery leaves can store fresh water. It has yellowish-green flowers in summer and autumn. If broken, the stem and leaves produce a poisonous juice.

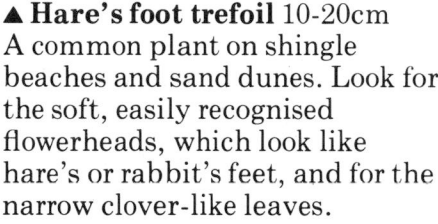

▲ **Seablite** 25-30cm
A small plant, common on salt-marshes, sandy and muddy shores. It doesn't mind being partly covered by sea-water and can even grow below the high-tide mark. It has thick fleshy leaves and tiny green flowers.

▲ **Hare's foot trefoil** 10-20cm
A common plant on shingle beaches and sand dunes. Look for the soft, easily recognised flowerheads, which look like hare's or rabbit's feet, and for the narrow clover-like leaves.

▲ **Viper's bugloss** 30-70cm
A very hairy plant which grows in dry gravelly places by the sea, and on limestone and chalk cliffs. The pink, trumpet-shaped flowers change to reddish-purple and then to brilliant blue.

▲**Sea storksbill** 5-15cm
A small, soft, hairy plant, which grows close to the ground. It has long pointed fruits, which look like the beaks of storks. It is common on sand dunes and dry wasteground near the sea.

▲ **Common orache** Up to 100cm
This large plant is common in waste places by the sea. Look for the thin red lines on the stem and the tiny green flowers, which have no petals. The plant can be boiled, like cabbage, and eaten.

▲ **Slender thistle** 15-75cm
A very prickly plant which grows on cliffs and waste ground near the sea. In summer it has clusters of tiny purple flowers at the end of each stem. There are spiny 'wings' running up the stems.

▲ **Thrift** or **Sea pink** 10-15cm
This common seaside plant is easy to recognize, and is often grown in gardens. The stiff, grass-like leaves grow together forming a thick cushion. In summer it has clusters of pale pink flowers, each cluster on a long stem.

Edible seaside plants
Several wild seaside plants have been cultivated to produce important food plants.

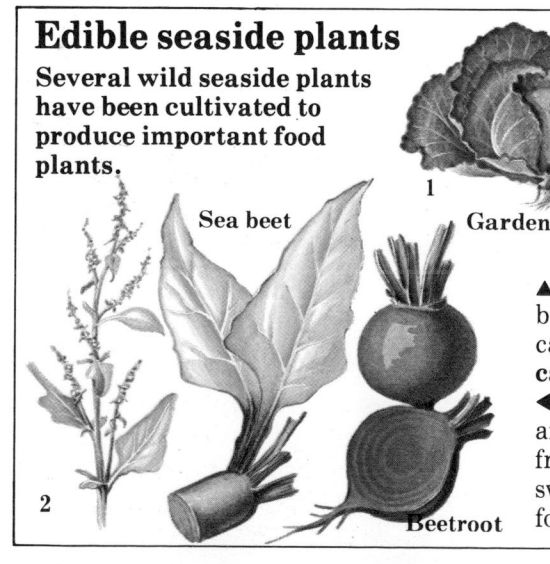

Sea beet

1 Garden cabbage

Sea cabbage

Beetroot

▲ **1 Garden cabbage**, broccoli, brussels sprouts and cauliflower all come from **sea cabbage** (right).
◄ **2 Beetroot**, sugar beet, and mangel wurzels all come from **sea beet** (left). The swollen root is the part used as food.

A salt-marsh

A salt-marsh is really a sheltered, low-lying area of land, soaked in seawater. The muddy soil is so salty that only certain plants and animals can survive the harsh conditions. Plants grow in bands or zones. Each zone is at a different height above sea-level. Salt-marshes are rich in birdlife. The birds search through muddy seawater creeks and pools for food.

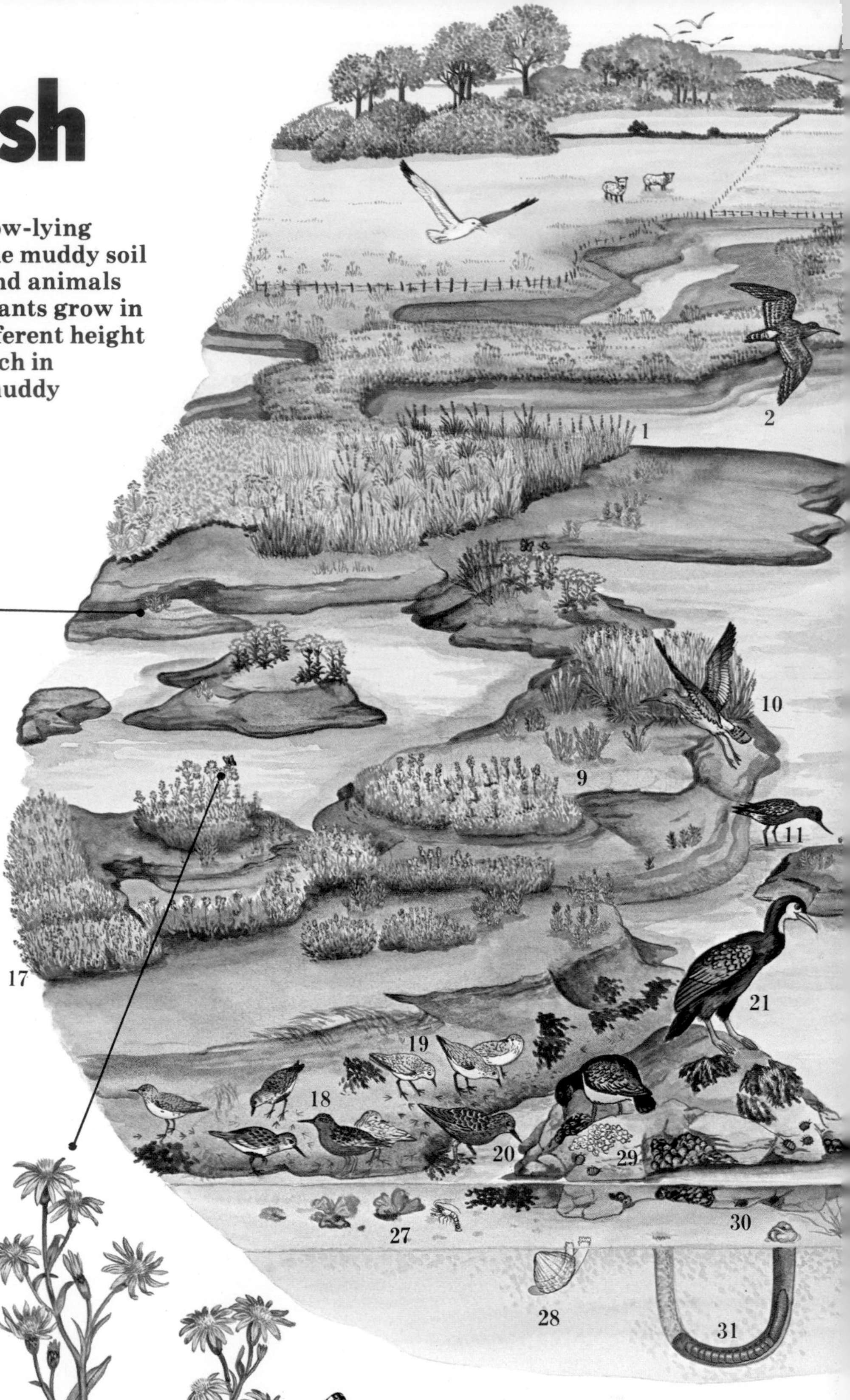

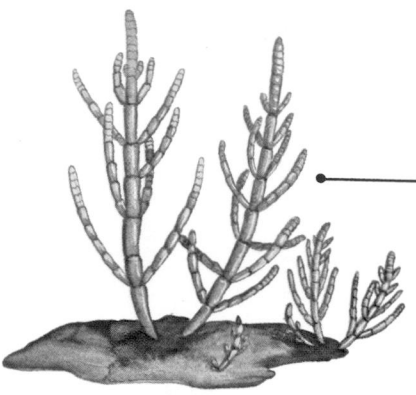

▲ Glasswort

Glasswort is a strange looking flowering plant. It has no leaves, and the tiny, green flowers have no petals. The fleshy, tubular stems can absorb and store fresh water. The roots are constantly in salt water but they can take in water without any salt.

Plants and levels

The fleshy spikes of glasswort (9) and the green bootlaces of eel grass (32) grow in the mud and are often covered by the tide. Mud is trapped between their stems and raises the level of the ground. Rice grass also traps mud with its roots.

Sea aster (8), sea purslane (17) and seablite (14) grow higher up, but are sometimes covered by the tide.

Well above high-tide level the spreading roots of sea meadow-grass (13) bind the muddy soil and make it firm. Whole areas may be carpeted with sea lavender (6). Cushions of thrift (5), shrubby sea purslane (17), and sea arrow-grass (1) are also common.

Painted lady butterfly

◀ Sea aster

Like most salt-marsh plants, the sea aster has fleshy water-storing leaves. It usually grows in large clumps, and its clusters of flowers brighten up the muddy creeks in late summer.

The painted lady butterfly has flown from North Africa to spend the summer in Europe.

▶ Rove beetles

At low tide, tiny rove beetles feed on algae and bits of rotting plants. They live in tunnels, which they dig at the top of muddy salt-marsh banks. Bubbles of air trapped in the tunnels help the beetles to survive if the tide rises too high.

Burrow entrance

Birds

Enormous numbers of waders, like Temminck's stint (26), dunlin (18) and godwits (11) poke about in the mud for small crustaceans and worms. At low tide, shelduck (24) hunt for snails, and eider duck (22) search for molluscs and crabs. The teal (23) feeds on glasswort.

Huge flocks of birds visit salt-marshes to feed, before flying on to winter homes or summer nesting sites.

▼ Flounders

Young flounders are found in muddy estuaries. When young they look like ordinary fish. As they get older, the left eye moves over to the right side of their flat bodies.

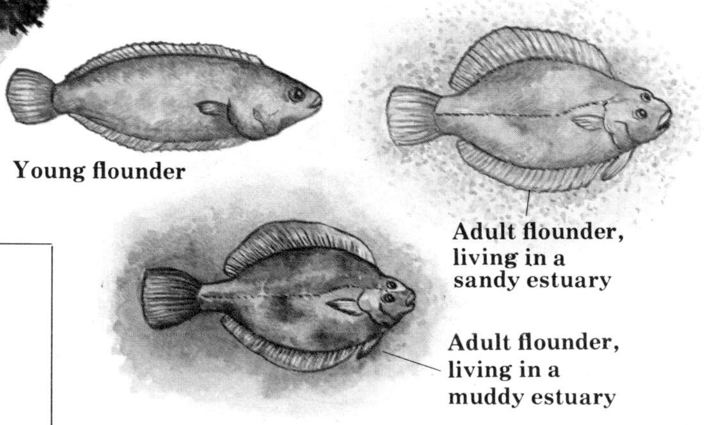

Young flounder

Adult flounder, living in a sandy estuary

Adult flounder, living in a muddy estuary

▲ The upper side of a flounder varies in colour to match the place where it lives. It feeds on cockles, crabs, shrimps and tiny fish, such as gobies.

Key

1 Sea arrow-grass	13 Sea meadow-grass	25 Oyster
2 Curlew	14 Seablite	26 Temminck's stint
3 Herring gull	15 Teal	27 Shrimp
4 Sea rush	16 Cord grass	28 Cockle
5 Thrift	17 Sea purslane	29 Barnacles
6 Sea lavender	18 Dunlin	30 Gribble
7 Heron	19 Sanderling	31 Lugworm
8 Sea aster	20 Knot	32 Eel grass
9 Glasswort	21 Cormorant	33 Ragworm
10 Redshank	22 Eider duck	34 Flounder
11 Godwit	23 Teal	35 Peppery furrow shell
12 Rove beetles	24 Shelduck	36 Shore crab

Fishes

There are not many fishes living on the shore, compared to the open sea. Most of them are found hiding among stones and weed in rock pools. Others bury themselves in mud or sand to avoid being seen and to stop themselves drying up when the tide is out. Sometimes shoals of sea fishes move into estuaries to feed, returning to the open sea to breed.

* Not to scale. Average body length given.

▲Common blenny 10-15cm
Very common in shallow rock pools. Using its fins, it is able to move short distances over rocks from one pool to another. It has a blunt head and large lips, and its body has no scales.

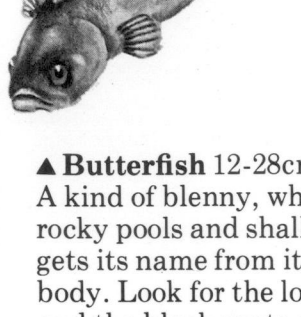

▲ Butterfish 12-28cm
A kind of blenny, which lives in rocky pools and shallow water. It gets its name from its slippery body. Look for the long dorsal fin, and the black spots circled with white along both sides of its body.

▲Worm pipefish 10-15cm
This little fish hides amongst brown seaweeds in rock pools and looks like a stiff brown straw. It is a poor swimmer, and feeds on small crustaceans. The eggs are carried on the male's abdomen until they hatch.

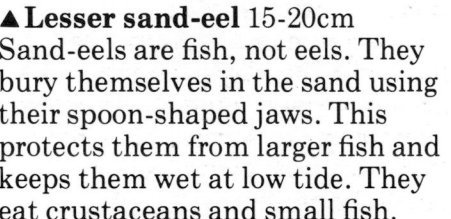

▲Lesser sand-eel 15-20cm
Sand-eels are fish, not eels. They bury themselves in the sand using their spoon-shaped jaws. This protects them from larger fish and keeps them wet at low tide. They eat crustaceans and small fish.

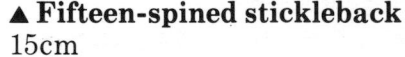

▲ Fifteen-spined stickleback 15cm
This is the only stickleback that lives in the sea. It hides under stones in pools, and has fifteen sharp spines on its back. In spring the male builds a nest for the eggs.

▲Sea scorpion 15-20cm
A small, fierce-looking fish, which lives in rock pools and shallow water. It catches small crustaceans with its enormous mouth. Look for the poisonous spines above the eye and on the gill covers.

▲Lesser weever fish 8-10cm
These fish live buried in the sand, and feed on shrimps. Spines on their backs inject poison into any animal that touches them or into you if you happen to tread on one! Be very careful if you go shrimping in bare feet.

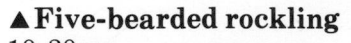

▲Five-bearded rockling 10-30cm
Rocklings belong to the cod family. This species has five sensitive whiskers around its mouth, which help it to find its food: worms, molluscs and crustaceans. It lives in rock pools.

▲ **Sand goby** 6-10cm
Very small fish which lives in
shallow sandy pools or rock pools.
Gobies are fast swimmers, but
when motionless they are almost
invisible. They feed on worms and
small crustaceans, like shrimps.

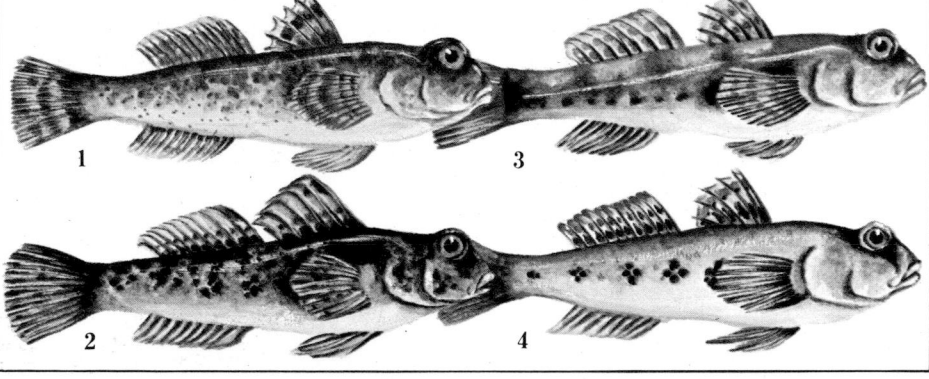

Some common gobies

You may see several different
gobies, as well as the sand
goby.
1 Rock goby: 10cm long
Lives on its own. Lurks under
stones in shallow rocky pools.

2 Black goby: 12cm
Quite common on muddy, rocky
and sandy shores.
3 Spotted goby: 8-10cm
Lives among oarweeds in deep
pools at the bottom of the shore.
4 Painted goby: 4cm
Found in sandy-bottomed pools.

▲ **Clingfish** 10cm
Small, scale-less fish with special
fins which form a large sucker.
This attaches the fish to rocks or
stones. The most common is the
Cornish suckerfish. During the
winter clingfishes move into deep
water.

▲ **Ballan wrasse** 20-25cm
These common, medium-sized
fish are brilliantly coloured. They
are sometimes found in seaweedy
pools on rocky shores. They have
thick lips and strong teeth to
crush the crustaceans and
molluscs on which they live.

▲ **Corkwing wrasse** 10-12cm
Sometimes called the 'sea-
partridge', this wrasse lives in
shallow pools. Wrasse build nests
from seaweed in which they lay
their eggs. They have an odd habit
of resting on their sides.

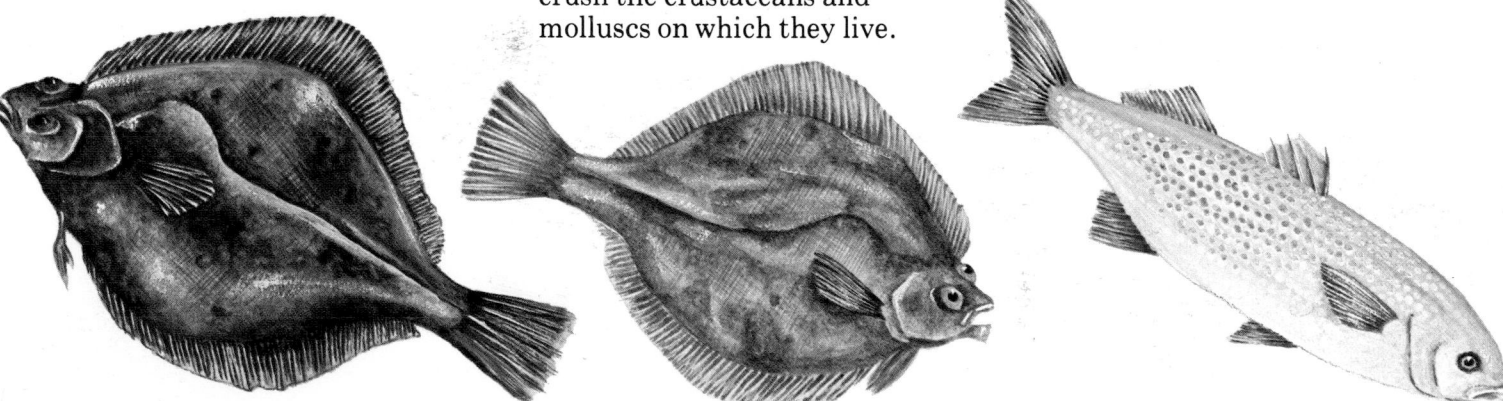

▲ **Dab** 10-25cm
Young dabs can often be found in
shallow water in sandy bays. They
are *flatfish*. This means that they
lie on one side with both eyes on the
upper surface. Dabs are a rounded
oval in shape and have rough
scales.

▲ **Flounder** 20-51cm
A common flatfish in muddy
estuaries and muddy or sandy
bays. It changes colour to match
its background, so that it is
difficult to see. On sandy shores it
is yellowish, but on mud it is dark
brown.

▲ **Grey mullet** 20-25cm
Shoals of young grey or 'thick-
lipped' mullet move into estuaries
from the sea to feed. They have no
teeth and mainly eat green algae
and sometimes small molluscs.
They return to the open sea to
breed.

The tides

What are tides?

The shore is covered with water twice in every 24 hours. The rise and fall of the water level is called a *tide*. Tides are caused by gravity – the same force that makes things fall. If there were no gravity the oceans would be spread out evenly over the earth. But the earth comes under the gravitational pull of both the sun and the moon.

Spring tides (diagram 1)

When the sun and moon are in line, their combined gravitational pull is large. This makes the waters pile up, and produces a very high tide. The earth itself is moved very slightly by this gravitational pull, and so there is another very high tide on the opposite side of the earth at the same time.

The high tides drain water from the sides of the earth away from the gravitational pull, so here there will be very low tides.

These very high and very low tides are called *spring tides*. The word *spring* has nothing to do with the season, but comes from a Norse word meaning 'swell'.

Neap tides (diagram 2)

When the sun and moon are not in line, the gravitational pull is not as strong. This causes less movement of the water and the tides are very small. These are called *neap tides*. *Neap* is another Norse word, and means 'scarcity'.

The time of tides

High tides happen when the moon is overhead. It is then that the gravitational pull is strongest. As the earth spins on its axis once every 24 hours, there is a high tide twice a day: once when the moon is overhead, and once when the moon is overhead on the opposite side of the earth.

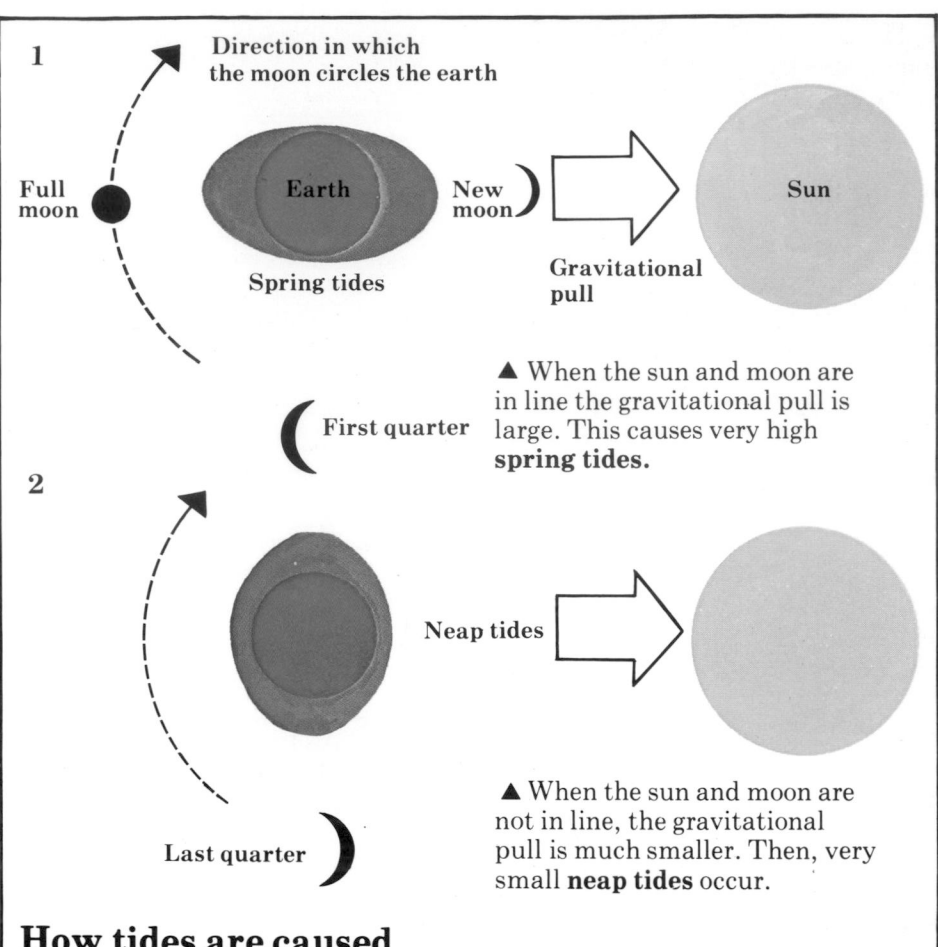

1 Direction in which the moon circles the earth

Full moon — Earth — New moon — Gravitational pull — Sun

Spring tides

2 First quarter

Neap tides

Last quarter

▲ When the sun and moon are in line the gravitational pull is large. This causes very high **spring tides.**

▲ When the sun and moon are not in line, the gravitational pull is much smaller. Then, very small **neap tides** occur.

How tides are caused

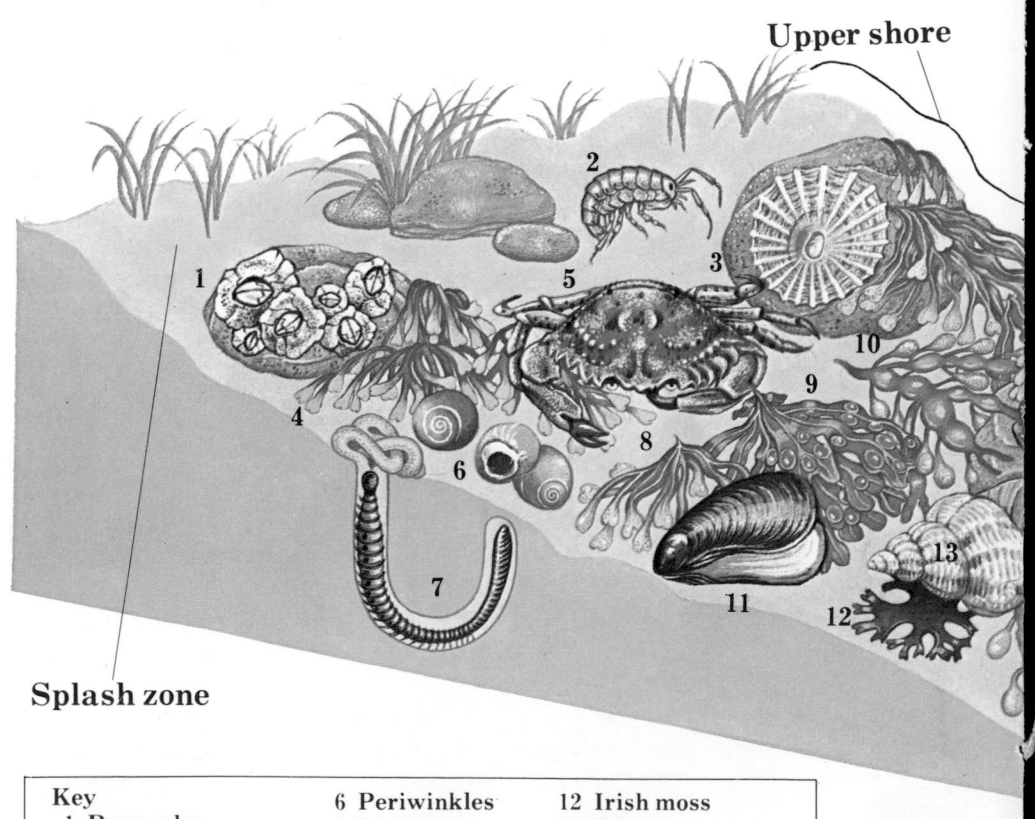

Upper shore

Splash zone

Key		
1 Barnacles	6 Periwinkles	12 Irish moss
2 Sandhopper	7 Lugworm	13 Whelk
3 Limpet	8 Spiral wrack	14 Beadlet anemone
4 Channelled wrack	9 Bladder wrack	15 Cockle
5 Shore crab	10 Egg wrack	16 Serrated wrack
	11 Mussel	17 Starfish

However, the moon circles the earth slightly slower than the earth spins on its axis. This means that high tides are at a slightly later time each day. If high tide is at 10.00am, in the morning, the next high tide will be at 10.25pm, in the evening – about 12 hours, 25 minutes later.

The movements of the earth, the sun and the moon are known. Therefore it is possible to know the times and the height of high tides at any place on the earth's surface. All this information is published in tide tables.

The height to which the tide rises varies everywhere along the coast, according to the type of coastline. In the Mediterranean the rise and fall may be as little as 15 centimetres, but around the coast of northern Europe it varies from about 2 metres to about 12 metres.

Life between the tides
The part of the shore covered and uncovered by the tide is called the *intertidal zone*.

The plants and animals in this zone have a difficult life. They are underwater for part of the time, but at other times they are left high and dry.

On a sloping beach the animals and plants at the bottom of the shore are covered by the sea most of the time. Those higher up the beach are underwater for about half the day. Those living right at the top may only be submerged a few times each month.

All animals and plants need water, so only those that are well protected against drying up can survive for any length of time on the upper shore. Those with less protection live lower down, in the middle shore zone, where they will be underwater for longer periods. The plants and animals which have little or no resistance to drying up live on the lower shore, which is almost always underwater.

Recognizing zones
You can see the zones in which different plants and animals live quite easily on a rocky shore.

You will also see *zonation* on tall rocks at low tide, and in rock pools.

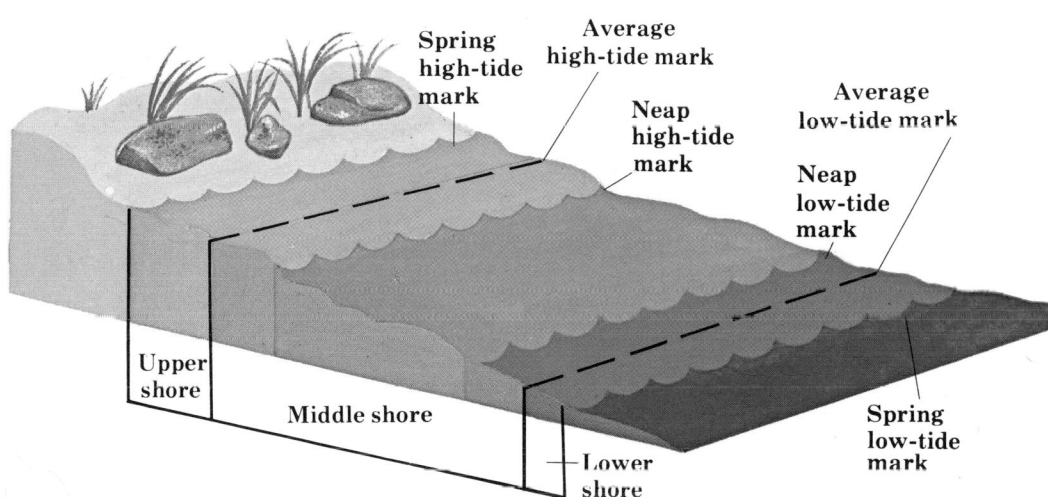

▲ The tides
This diagram shows the points reached by different tides. The palest blue area is hardly ever underwater. The darkest blue area is always underwater.

The highest spring tides and the lowest neap tides happen twice a month. After a spring tide, the tide level changes a little each day until the neap tide level is reached. After the neap tide, the rise and fall slowly increases until the spring levels are reached.

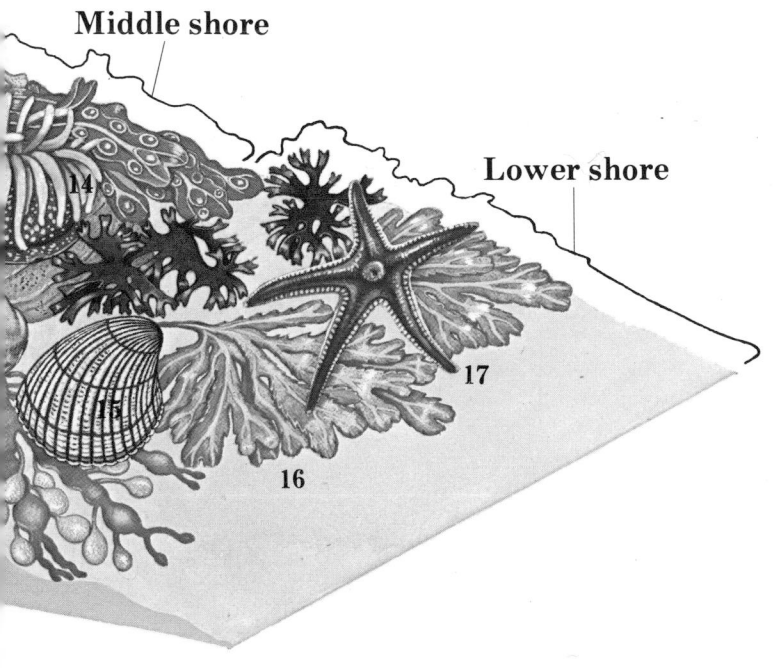

◀ The zones on a shore
The shore can be divided into zones. The *splash zone* is kept damp with salt spray. The *upper shore zone* is from the highest spring tide to the average high-tide mark. It is uncovered for long periods. The large *middle shore zone* stretches between the average high tide and average low-tide point. This zone is rich in animals and plants. The *lower shore zone* is from the average low tide to the lowest spring-tide mark. This zone is not exposed to the air very often. Together, the three zones are known as the *intertidal zone*.

Particular animals and plants live in each zone. Some of the most common ones are shown here (not drawn to scale).

Rocks and pebbles

Different kinds of seashore

When you go to a beach, it may be made of rocks and pebbles, shingle, sand or mud. But all of them are made up from bits of rock.

Shingle beaches are made up of large stones and smaller pebbles. The sand grains on sandy beaches are much smaller pieces of soft rock. Muddy shore rock particles are so tiny that dry mud is a soft powder.

Where do all these bits of rock come from? Why are there different kinds of beach?

From rock to mud

Sand, shingle and pebbles were once larger rocks. They may have been part of a seashore cliff, or part of a mountain inland.

Wherever rocks come from, they are broken down into smaller pieces by a process called 'weathering'. The diagram below shows some of the ways in which rocks are weathered.

Rocks are broken into smaller pieces by heat, cold and rain. These pieces fall, or are carried downwards by streams. The streams join up to form rivers, carrying rocks with them. The rocks are tumbled and battered, becoming more rounded and smaller.

When the pebbles reach the sea they may be carried far away by the currents, until they are washed up on beaches. Here they join the pebbles which have been formed by the action of the wind and waves on the seashore cliffs.

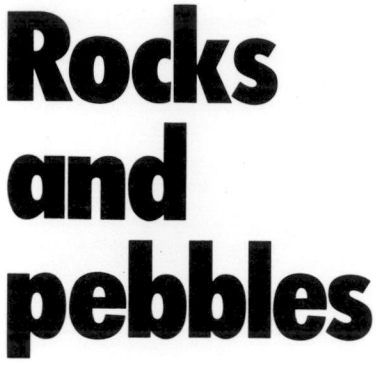

1 Mountain boulders are split by heat, cold and rain. Water in cracks expands as it freezes, splitting the rocks.

2 Rainwater finds its way down through cracks and forms streams. These join up to form rivers.

3 Rocks are split by plant roots. Animal burrows allow water and air to reach cracks in underground rocks.

4 The rocks break up. Pieces fall into streams and rivers below.

5 The rocks become smooth and rounded as they are carried towards the sea.

6 When they reach the sea, the smallest pieces of rock settle on sheltered beaches or mud-flats. Larger pieces may be carried along the coast before they are washed up on a beach as pebbles.

Rocky shores
Hard rocky shores are often made from volcanic rock. There are usually no high cliffs, even though many of the rocks may be quite steep, and jagged. You will find the best rock pools on these beaches.

Look for slate, granite and quartz pebbles, like the ones in the picture on the right. You may also find gneiss and schists. These are rocks which have been melted, folded and squeezed as they were formed. If you look carefully you will see many tiny swirling folds in these rocks.

Soft rocky beaches, made of limestone, have high steep cliffs. The waves wear away the rocks to form a fairly flat beach, often with limestone and flint pebbles.

Pebbly beaches
Shingle beaches are usually found on shores which are exposed to high winds and stormy seas. The rocks are battered and tumbled, and become smooth and rounded. Most of the pebbles on this kind of beach come from local rocks, but some will have been carried from far away by rivers and sea currents.

In northern Europe, pebbles were moved thousands of kilometres by glaciers during the Ice Age.

Pebbles are also moved along the coast by seaweeds. Some seaweeds, such as oarweed, attach themselves to large pebbles. The seaweeds float, and the pebbles are bumped along the sea-bed for many kilometres before being cast up on the beach.

Sandy beaches
Sand grains are formed by soft rocks breaking down. They are lighter than pebbles so they will only settle in sheltered places.

This is why sandy beaches are usually in sheltered bays. If there are sandstone cliffs behind the beach they will be worn away by the wind and waves, adding more sand to the beach.

Muddy shores
Mud is formed from the tiniest particles of rock. They will only settle in the most sheltered places. This is why muddy beaches are usually found in sheltered estuaries.

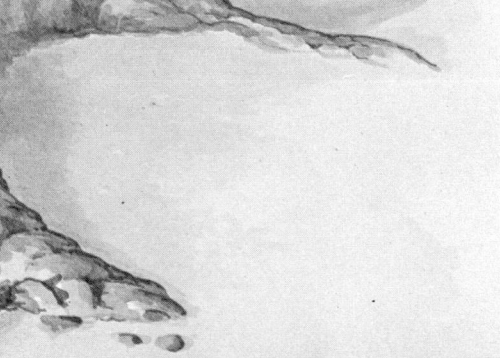

Some common pebbles

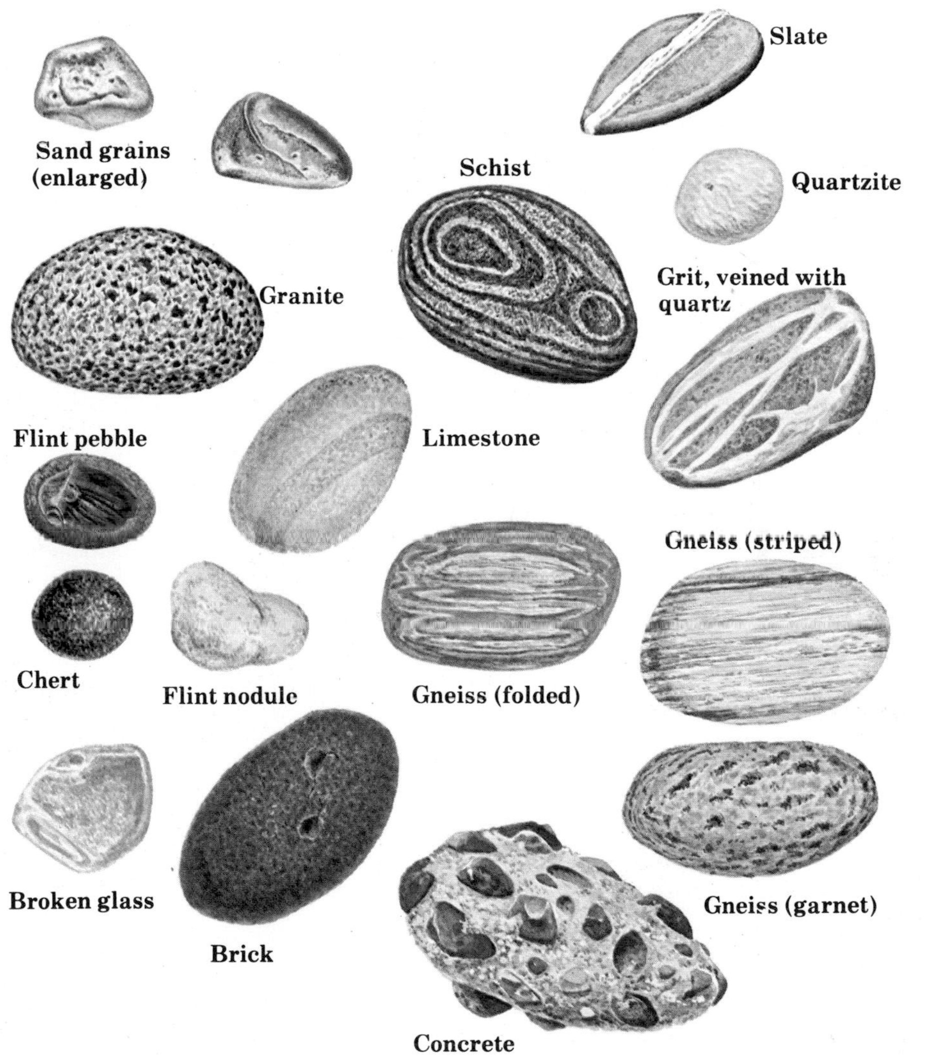

Sand grains (enlarged)

Slate

Schist

Quartzite

Granite

Grit, veined with quartz

Flint pebble

Limestone

Chert

Flint nodule

Gneiss (folded)

Gneiss (striped)

Broken glass

Brick

Concrete

Gneiss (garnet)

Semi-precious stones

Onyx pebble, weathered by the sea

Amethyst crystals

Cut onyx, set in a ring

Polished amethyst, set in earrings

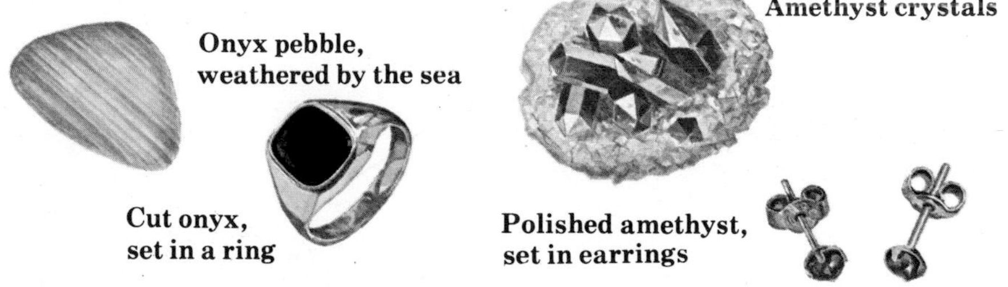

Beach-combing

Where to look

At the top of the shore, near or above the high-tide mark, there is usually a line of dead seaweed and rubbish thrown up by the waves. This is called the *strandline*. If you look carefully among the seaweed you will find many interesting things.

Life on the strandline

If you disturb the dry seaweed at the top of the beach, hundreds of sandhoppers will leap out or wriggle away to safety. They are crustaceans, like crabs, and they feed on rotting seaweed and animal remains. Gulls, turnstones, beetles and flies also search through the strandline rubbish for food.

Animal remains

Look for the shells and pincers of crabs, and for empty mollusc shells. You may find spongy masses of yellow polystyrene-like bubbles. These are the egg-cases of the common whelk.

Fishes are sometimes stranded by the tide, and the empty egg-cases or 'mermaid's purses' of the skate and dogfish are common.

Rules
Protect the seashore by following these simple rules.
1 Never dig up plants or pick their flowers.
2 Return animals that you have caught to the same place as soon as possible.
3 Be careful not to be cut off by the tide.
4 Never eat anything you find on a beach (dead or alive).
5 Take your litter home.
6 Watch, but do not disturb, the plants and animals if at all possible.

▶ Magnified section through gribble-bored wood, showing the animal in its tunnel. The gribble is a crustacean.

▼ Magnified section through teredo-bored wood, showing the animal in its burrow. The teredo, or shipworm, is a bivalve mollusc.

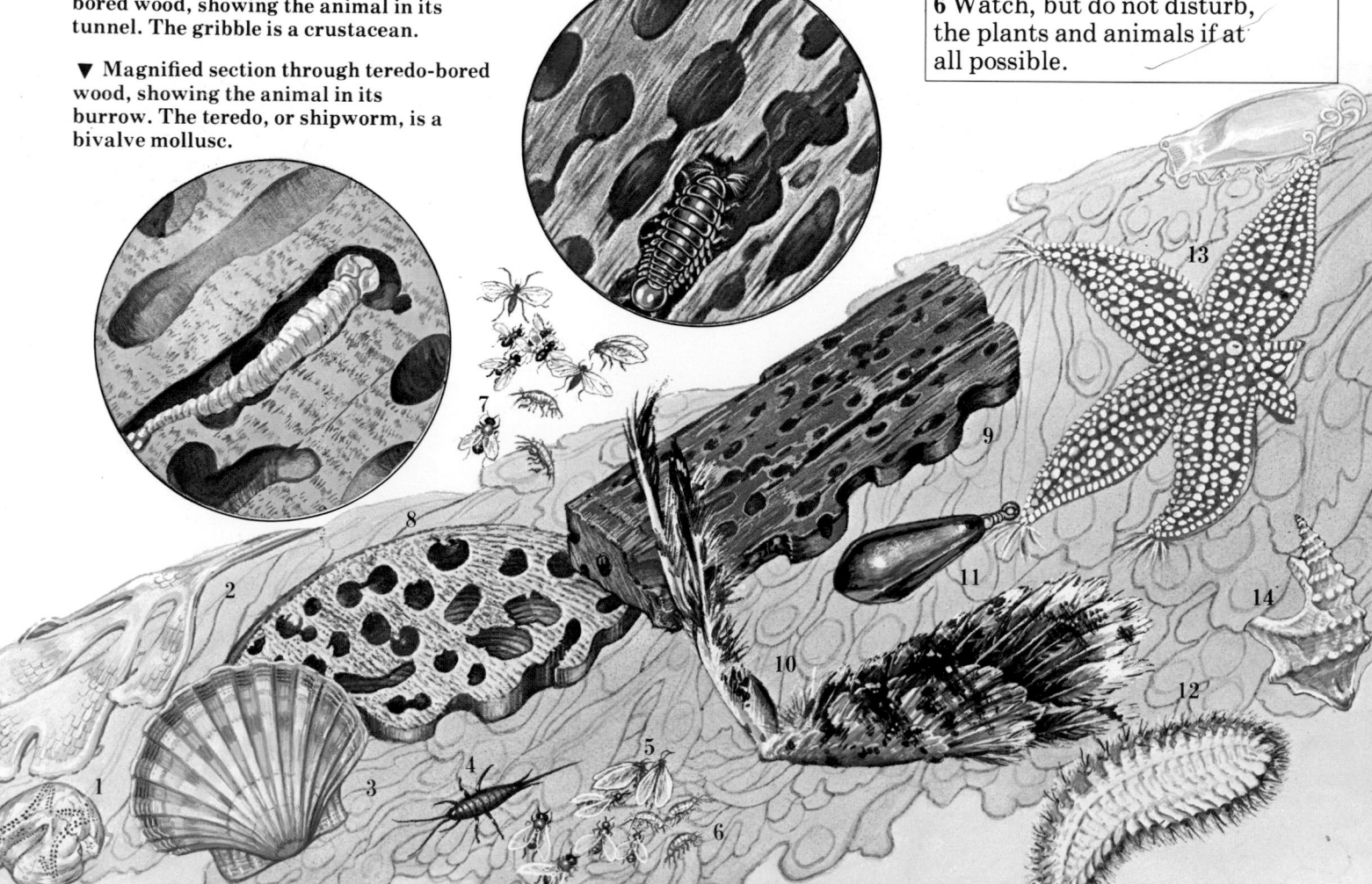

Chalky white cuttlefish bones come from an animal like an octopus. If you see a tiny hairy object, glinting green and gold, this will be a dead sea-mouse.

The sad corpses of oiled seabirds are far too common. Most of them are killed by swallowing oil as they try to clean their feathers. Jellyfishes are sometimes stranded on a beach. Be careful not to touch them as they have a powerful sting.

Sea sculpture

Wood floats, so is often washed up by the tide. Some has been worn into beautiful shapes by the sea. It is often riddled with holes. Small holes may be the tunnels of a tiny crustacean called a gribble.

Larger holes may have been made by shipworms. Strip off the wood carefully with a penknife to find this bivalve in its burrow.

Artificial objects

Look for cork and plastic fishing floats, rope and nets. Ships use the sea as a dustbin. Instead of sinking, their rubbish often floats and comes ashore. Bottles, tins, boxes and crates may have labels from many different countries.

Scientists often fix a small metal tag to an animal, such as a fish or a bird, to follow its movements. If you find one, send it to the address printed on the tag, enclosing a note of where and when you found the tag.

People leave a lot of litter on beaches. Look out for jagged tins, broken bottles and even sharp plastic cutlery. Don't leave *your* litter on the beach!

How to look

If you search *carefully* and *slowly* on a beach, or sit *quietly* by the side of a rock-pool, you will see many of the animals and plants in this book. Some animals are very shy and only come out when they think you have gone away, so you must be *quiet* and *patient*. Remember – this is their home, so don't destroy it.

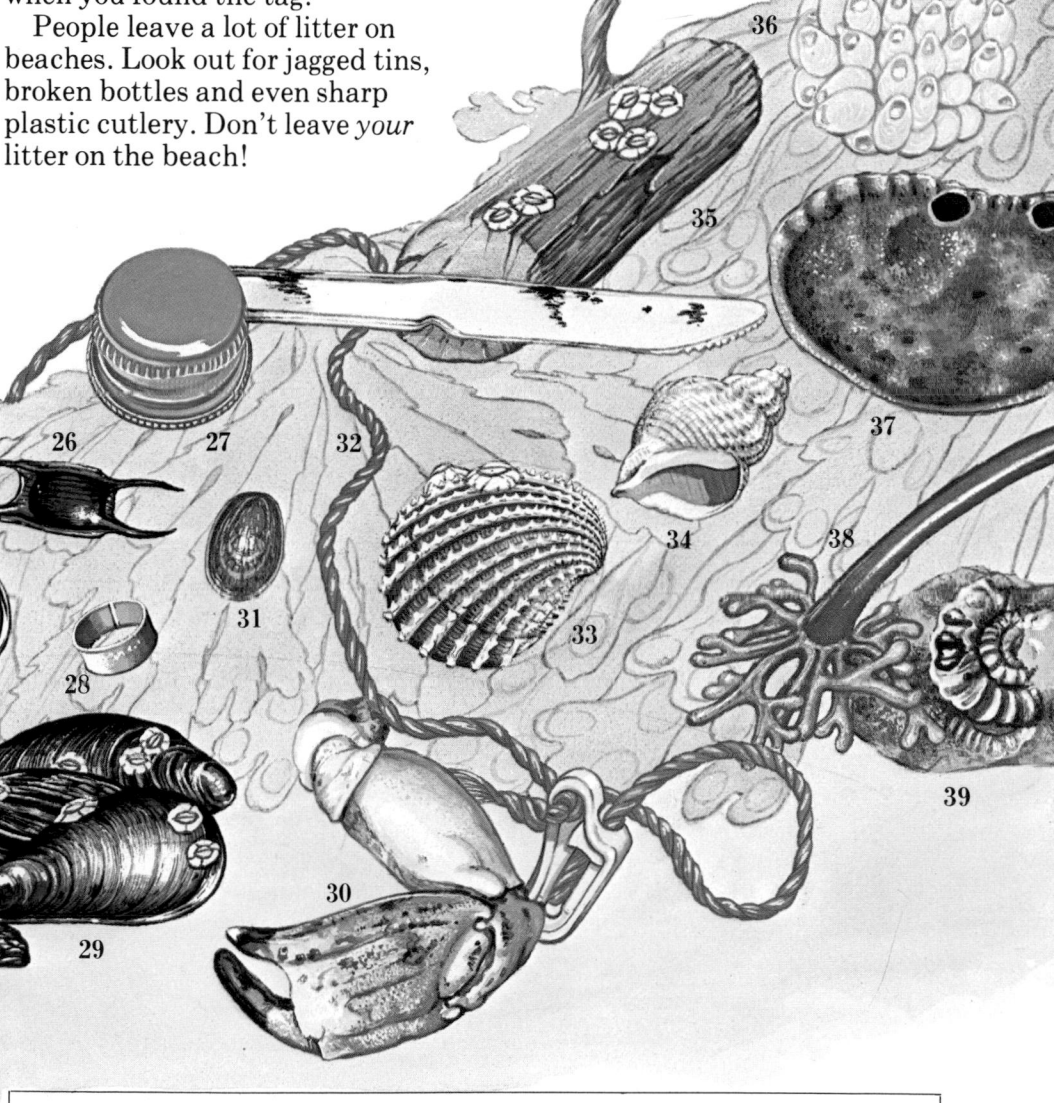

Key		
1 Sea-potato test	13 Damaged starfish	26 Mermaid's purse
2 Hornwrack	14 Pelican's foot shell	27 Bottle-top
3 Scallop shell	15 Dead shore crabs	28 Bird tag
4 Bristletail	16 Cowrie	29 Mussels
5 Seaweed flies	17 Barnacles	30 Edible-crab claw
6 Sandhoppers	18 Painted topshell	31 Blue-rayed limpet
7 Seaweed midges	19 Flat topshell	32 Rope
8 Teredo-bored wood	20 Cuttlefish bone	33 Spiny cockle shell
9 Gribble-bored wood	21 Part of an oiled detergent	34 Whelk shell
10 Part of a dead, oiled	bottle	35 Driftwood
seabird	22 Periwinkles	36 Whelk egg-cases
11 Net weight	23 Fishing net	37 Crab shell
12 Sea-mouse	24 Cork	38 Holdfast from oarweed
	25 Fish-hook	39 Part of an ammonite fossil

41

Word list

Algae: A group of simple non-flowering plants. All the seaweeds are algae. There are also many freshwater and land algae. Algae are divided into groups according to their colour. The brown algae include bladderwrack and saw wrack. Sea lettuce is a green alga.

Bivalve: A mollusc with two shells, which are joined by a hinge. The pod razor, mussel, oyster and cockle are all bivalves.

Community: A group of plants and animals living together in the same habitat. Some of the organisms depend on the other members of the community as a source of food.

Crustaceans: Invertebrates that live mainly in the water. They have a hard outside skeleton (shell), breathe through gills and have two pairs of antennae (feelers). Barnacles, crabs, shrimps and lobsters are all crustaceans. The sea slater is a crustacean which can live out of water in the splash zone.

Echinoderm: A spiny-skinned animal with many tube-feet. The body often has five arms. Starfish and sea-urchins are echinoderms.

Erosion: The wearing away of rocks and soil by water and wind.

Habitat: The natural surroundings in which a plant or animal lives.

Intertidal zone: The part of the shore that is covered and uncovered by the tide twice a day.

Invertebrate: An animal without a backbone. Sea-anemones, insects, spiders, crustaceans, molluscs and echinoderms are all invertebrates.

Larva: A young stage in the life cycle of many animals. The larva of the sand-wasp hatches from the egg. The larva of the cinnabar moth is called a caterpillar. The caterpillar is the stage in an insect life history between the egg and the pupa.

Mermaid's purse: The egg-case of the dogfish or skate.

Mollusc: An invertebrate animal with a hard chalky shell and muscular 'foot'. Limpets, cockles and topshells are all molluscs. Most molluscs are slow moving. Cuttlefish and octopus are highly developed molluscs. The shell is beneath the leathery skin. They have well developed eyes and long arms with suckers. They are fast moving.

Moulting: When a crab or lobster has outgrown its rigid outer skeleton, the shell splits and the animal wriggles out. Underneath, a new, soft skeleton has formed. This gradually hardens to a larger size, giving the animal more room to grow.
   Many invertebrates, particularly crustaceans and insects, will moult several times during their lives.

Pupa: A stage in insect development between larva and adult. The pupa, which has a hard covering, does not feed and stays almost motionless. Inside, great changes take place. Wings and legs develop and the larva changes into an adult. The cinnabar moth, sand-wasp and solitary bee all go through pupal stages in their life history.

Splash zone: The area at the top of the shore which is kept damp by the splashes and spray from the waves.

Strandline: A line of dead seaweed and rubbish at the top of the shore. It is usually found at the high-tide mark.

Test: The shell of an echinoderm, such as a sea-urchin.

Tide: The regular rise and fall of the water, covering and uncovering the shore twice a day. Spring tides are the highest and lowest tides. Neap tides are the smallest tides.

Vertebrate: Animal with a backbone. Fishes, amphibians, reptiles, birds and mammals are all vertebrates.

Wader: Birds which walk about in shallow water looking for food such as worms and molluscs. They are often found in large flocks on estuaries and salt-marshes. Curlews, redshanks and knots are all waders.

Weathering: The breaking down of rocks into smaller stones, pebbles, sands, silt and clays. Wind, rain, frost, the sun's heat, chemical reactions and burrowing animals all help to weather the rocks.

How to find out more

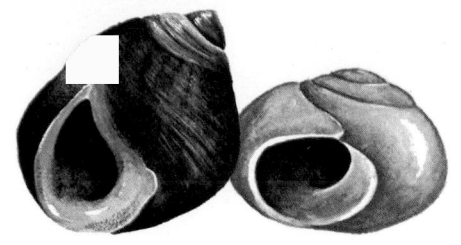

Clubs

One way of finding out more is to join a club. There are several different ones with junior sections, which will help you learn more about seashore habitats. Always enclose a stamped addressed envelope when you write for information.

You can get the addresses of your local **Natural History Society** and local **County Naturalist Trust** from
Council for Environmental Conservation
c/o The Zoological Society
Regent's Park
London NW1 4RY

The **British Naturalists' Association** has a quarterly magazine with a special section for junior members. For more information write to
Mrs Y. Griffiths
23 Oak Hill Close
Woodford Green
Essex 1GP 9PH

The **Royal Society for the Protection of Birds (RSPB)** has a junior branch, the **Young Ornithologists' Club (YOC)**. You can belong to this if you are under 15. It arranges outings and meetings, and produces a magazine called *Bird Life*. This contains articles by experts and members, information on competitions and projects, and club news. Members also receive a membership card and badge. For more information and an enrolment form write to
YOC
The Lodge
Sandy
Bedfordshire

The **Watch Club** is run by the *Sunday Times* and the **County Nature Conservation Trust**. It is for 10 to 15 year-olds and organizes projects and other activities. One recent activity was to invent an easy way of measuring water pollution. Membership is very cheap, and members receive the magazine, *Watchword*, three times a year. For more information write to
Watch
22 The Green
Nettleham
Lincoln LN2 2NR

The **Wildlife Youth Service** is a branch of the World Wildlife Fund. It organises various conservation-based activities. Write to
Marston Court
98-106 Manor Road
Wallington
Surrey

If you find bird rings or tags send them *either* to the address on the ring or tag *or* to
British Trust for Ornithology
Beech Grove
Station Road
Tring
Herts.

Use the **Local Information Centres** that are set up in many seaside towns. They may be able to suggest which beaches are best for rockpools, shell collecting or bird watching. They will also be able to advise you about tides and which beaches are safe to visit. They will have information about local cliff walks.

You will also find **National Trust Centres** where there are National Trust coastal paths. These give detailed information about the local coastline and the animals and plants you may find there.

The **Field Studies Council** runs field centres, many of which organize guided walks in the summer months. Some of these walks include bird-watching and visiting the local beach. Write to
9 Devereux Court
London WC2

Many seaside towns have a marine aquarium, containing living specimens of animals that you may find on the beach. Because the animals are underwater, you can see them moving about and feeding.

Don't forget to visit local seaside museums. These often contain many interesting specimens, rocks and fossils found on the local beaches. Other exhibits may tell you more about the history of the local beaches and how they have changed over the years.

Books

Further reading
There are hundreds of books about European wildlife. Those listed here are only a very small selection. Visit your local **bookshops** and **libraries** to find what else is available.

If you are not already a member of the local library, it would be an excellent idea for you to join.

General information books
Seashore (Black's Picture Information Books) Ian Murray (A & C Black). Covers identification and relationships on the seashore.
Naturetrail Book of Seashore Life Su Swallow (Usborne). Collecting activities, identification.

The Seashore C. M. Yonge (Collins) Very readable, standard reference work for older children.
The World of an Estuary Heather Angel (Faber) Explores the residents, visitors and habitat.
Crabs, Shells and Gulls (Wild Life Studies series) (Basil Blackwell). Detailed information for younger children; good illustrations.
Exploring the Seashore Leslie Jackman (Evans). Good general survey.
Understanding the Sea (Ladybird). Simple introduction to aspects of sea and seashore life.

Identification

Pocket Guide to the Seashore C.M. Yonge (Collins) Excellent general identification book.
Young Specialist looks at: Seashore; Marine Life Kosch, Freiling and Janus (Burke). Quite detailed identification books written in an understandable way. There are keys, descriptions and pictures.
Seashore and Shallow Seas of Britain and Europe; Shells of the World (Hamlyn Guides). Two excellent guides with clear pictures and short but rather scientific descriptions. Highly recommended.
Seashore Life in Colour Gwynne Vevers (Blandford). Good, clear pictures of all kinds of seashore creatures. The descriptions at the back of the book also include information about the structure of the organisms.
Fishes of the Sea, the Coastal Waters of the British Isles, Northern Europe and the Mediterranean John and Gillian Lythgoe (Blandford). A good identification book.
Coast, Estuary and Seashore Alan Major (John Gifford). An excellent book all about seashores. The descriptions of the plants and animals are easy to read and understand.
Spotters Guides: Seashore; Fishes; Birds; Butterflies; Wild Flowers; Rocks and Minerals (Usborne). Small, cheap and great fun to read.
The Oxford Book of: Invertebrates; Vertebrates; Insects; Birds; Wild Flowers; Flowerless Plants (Oxford University Press). These guides have good, clear pictures to help in identification and simple, easy to follow descriptions.

Observer books: *Sea and Seashore; Shells; Geology; Birds; Wild Flowers* (Warne). Small, easy to use reference books with a little background information.
Birds of Sea and Coast Jonsson; *Rocks and Pebbles of Britain and Northern Europe* Ostergaard/Whittow and Jensen (Penguin Nature Guides). Very good background information.

Birds

Coloured Key to Wildfowl of the World Peter Scott (Wildfowl Trust). This book identifies every duck, goose and swan you are ever likely to come across.
Field Guide to Birds of Britain and Europe Peterson, Mountfort and Hollom (Collins). A detailed bird guide.
RSPB Guide to Birdwatching (RSPB/Mitchell Beazley). Some helpful hints.
The RSPB Guide to British Birds D. Saunders (Hamlyn). Some good illustrations.
Birds of Britain and Europe Bertel Bruun (Hamlyn). Excellent reference book.
Birds Neil Ardley (Macdonald New Reference Library). Good introduction to bird life.

Flowering plants

Pocket Encyclopaedia of Wild Flowers in Colour; Wildflowers of Britain M.S. Christiansen Phillips (Pan). Good, clear pictures and descriptions.
Collins Guide to Wild Flowers (Collins). Standard reference book.
Hamlyn Concise Guides; Wild Flowers; Grasses (Hamlyn). Useful reference books.
Wild Flowers (Octopus). Classified by flower colour.

Rocks and minerals

Rocks and Minerals (Ladybird). A simple introduction to some common rocks and minerals.
Minerals, Rocks and Fossils Hamilton, Wooley, Bishop (Hamlyn Guide). Good photographs.
Minerals and Rocks in Colour; Fossils in Colour (Blandford). Good identification book in colour.
Pebbles on the Beach C. Ellis (Faber). An interesting book that tells you all about pebbles.

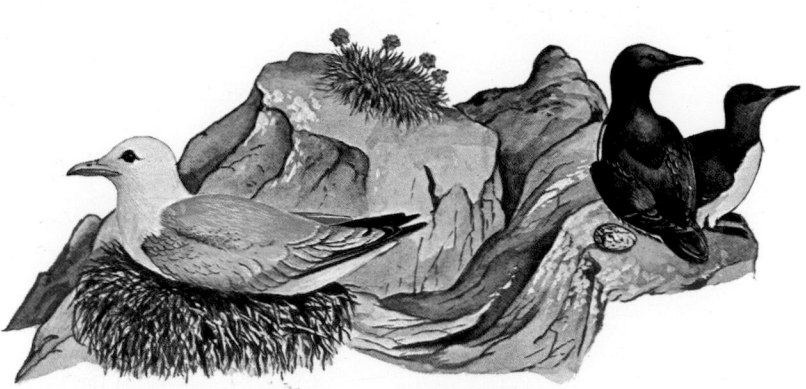

Index

Numbers in **bold** refer to illustrations.